REVIVAL

IN OUR TIME

᷃

The Story of the

BILLY GRAHAM

Evangelistic Campaigns

᷃

Including Six of His Sermons

The Publishers express their appreciation to all who
cooperated with them in the preparation of this book

Special Edition for

Northwestern Schools

50 Willow on Loring Park, Minneapolis 3, Minnesota

Published by

Van Kampen Press

Wheaton, Ill.

Great, Heart-Warming Days

I BELIEVE we are seeing the first indications of a coming mighty revival in America, for certainly the iniquities of our land have all but separated our people from God. "When the enemy shall come in like a flood the spirit of the Lord shall lift up a standard against him."

God is using chosen vessels throughout the country in comparatively small, but most encouraging ways, and truly revival sparks are flying. But among many others, God seems to have chosen Dr. William Graham, affectionately known as "Billy," to do an outstanding—even spectacular work—in starting revival fires, as attested in the recent campaigns in Los Angeles and Boston.

Billy Graham is a man after my own heart, for God's work. He can be trusted! He is a humble, prayerful, consecrated young man who seeks earnestly to work in God's way that his ministry may be owned of the Holy Spirit. I could see no fleshly methods in his ministry. As I attended his meetings in Los Angeles night after night he poured out, preaching, warning, exhorting, with great natural ability and with the power of the Holy Spirit. He is a man of prayer. He wants God and God alone to have all the glory.

In the Los Angeles campaign Billy had excellent helpers in Mr. and Mrs. Barrows and Beverly Shea and others. The Christian Business Men's Committee of Los Angeles stood by most faithfully all during the months of preparation, organizing hundreds of prayer meetings, fighting through all of the Satanic opposition. All working together they greatly rejoiced as they and I saw scores of people come up the aisles as the invitation was given night after night—some weeping and under great

3

conviction—all filed into the prayer room, seeking forgiveness for sins, becoming new creatures in Christ Jesus.

In Los Angeles a good many from the entertainment world were reached and some nationally-known figures were won for Christ. All sorts of people, old and young, rich and poor, filed up those aisles of sawdust after Billy had poured out heart and soul, warning of eternal separation if Christ is rejected but making plain the way to accept God's gift of eternal life.

Those were great, heart-warming days in Los Angeles! May a like harvest be reaped all over the country by Billy Graham and others like him who humbly and sincerely preach Christ in the power of the Holy Spirit. *Charles E. Fuller, The Old Fashioned Revival Hour, Los Angeles, California.*

Revival Visits Boston

GOD HAS broken through the crust of conservative, cultured, and intellectual Boston through the preaching of Billy Graham. Not since the revival days of Billy Sunday has anything happened in Boston comparable to this. Thousands have been converted and tens of thousands have heard the gospel preached in power.

For years many of us have labored, prayed and worked for God to send revival to this arid wilderness in theological things. Now God has answered our prayers and set the revival fires to burning.

Young Billy Graham came as the guest of Park Street Church to hold a church meeting, but immediately it was evident that God had come before him and prepared the way. The church proved too small on the second night, and the largest halls in Boston were used until in eighteen days 105,000 people had attended the meetings. There can be no explanation of this phenomenal movement outside of the supernatural. The glory must go to God not the evangelist (although he is definitely the human instrument used of God in these services), not to the sponsoring church, not to the workers, not to the times, but only to God must be given the praise for this revival.

The universal impression among the Christians in this area is that America's revival is breaking, and we praise God that it has struck Boston in the early part of the great campaign. *Harold J. Ockenga, Pastor, Park Street Church, Boston, Mass.*

I Was There

I SAW 15,000 people present in the Boston Gardens the last night of the tremendous Billy Graham revival. I heard him preach on the steps where thousands stood endeavoring to get into the service. I saw and heard a great choir of 3,500 voices; the special music was beyond compare. I heard the Spirit anointed preacher explain the plan of salvation to the great throng. I saw his compassionate heart revealed as he stood in the breach, giving the invitation, pleading with people to turn to God. I saw 1500 people make professions of faith in one single service. I saw the personal workers and the ministers, who had charge of the revival work, in the inquiry room with these hundreds. It was the mightiest demonstration of spiritual power which these eyes of mine have ever beheld. I found myself praying that Dr. Billy Graham might be the hot point to spearhead the great revival so sorely needed in America. A repetition of the Boston revival is the imperative need in all America today. *C. Wade Freeman, Supt., Department of Evangelism, The Baptist General Convention of Texas.*

CONTENTS

TASTING REVIVAL—at *Los Angeles*

by Mel Larson

BILLY GRAHAM was 30 years of age on September 25, 1949, when he stepped onto the platform of a mammoth canvas cathedral tent at Los Angeles, California's Christ for Greater Los Angeles' annual evangelistic campaign.

Eight weeks later when he walked off the platform of that canvas cathedral whose seating capacity had been swelled to 9,000, Billy Graham had celebrated a birthday and was 31 years of age.

But a mere birthday celebration was insignificant when compared to what that six-foot-two-inch young American evangelist had seen and experienced in those eight weeks.

Revival flowed through Billy Graham during that time until the entire world was conscious of it.

David Morken in Shanghai, China, working for Christ through Youth for Christ behind the bamboo curtain, picked up his Communist-censored newspaper one day and read on page one of the revival campaign in Los Angeles, California.

Millions of people in England paused in their restricted ways to read in the *London Illustrated* (the Britisher's LIFE magazine) of an unusual spiritual outpouring in Los Angeles, Calif. (They did not know that one of their reporters had talked by transatlantic phone to Graham for 15 minutes in getting a first-hand report of it).

In Switzerland, an American lady missionary working in a Bible school picked up a German-language magazine full of pictures and read with keen interest of unusual spiritual meetings in California, U.S.A. Right in the middle of the extensive write-up was a large picture of Billy Graham and a platform scene showing Cliff Barrows leading the singing.

9

Across America from coast to coast and from Canada to the gulf, newspapers readers saw in an Associated Press of November 2, 1949, the story of a new rising evangelist who "tops Billy Sunday." In their November 14, 1949, issue of *Time* magazine they read in their religion department that ". . . Graham seemed to be wielding the revival sickle as no one since Billy Sunday had wielded it. . . ." For 14½ inches of type and photograph they read of the moving of the Holy Spirit in the city of the angels.

On November 16, 1949, the millions of readers of LIFE magazine paused in their weekend reading to look at four pages of pictures of "A RISING YOUNG EVANGELIST." Readers *of Newsweek, Quick* and other magazines paused to read with wonder and interest of a man who had stirred Los Angeles and its film neighbor Hollywood as perhaps no churchman had stirred it for a generation.

Nothing perhaps has gripped the thinking of religious—and secular—Americans as did the revival campaign in Los Angeles in the autumn of 1949. Dr. Wilbur Smith of Pasadena, Calif., noted Bible scholar and theologian, appraised it in these words: "I have no doubt but that this is the most important evangelistic meeting in America this year." Others who were privileged to view the campaign and analyze it, readily agreed.

But just what *did* happen at Los Angeles from September 25 through November 20, 1949?

What was it that caused the hearts of Christians around the world to change their general revival praying into something specific as they looked at one another and said, "Perhaps it's here!"

What was it that catapulted the 31-year-old president of Northwestern Schools in Minneapolis and the vice-president of Youth for Christ International into international limelight?

So many other questions come to mind. Why this, why that? How this, how that? When did it start, who was behind it?

It may seem trite to say it, but it, of course, must be said. God was in it.

To be sure, God had been in previous campaigns sponsored by Clifford Smith's far-seeing, vision-filled Christ for Greater Los Angeles campaign committee. God had been with Billy Graham as he spearheaded the Youth for Christ work as it forged its dynamic way into 59 countries of the world. God had been in the work of Billy and his co-workers, Cliff and Billie Barrows, in six rugged months in England in the winter of 1946 and 1947 when campaign after campaign resulted in the needed formation of British Youth for Christ.

God had been in the adding of baritone soloist George Beverly Shea to the team in the summer of 1949 to round out the three-man group. God had been with them in city-wide campaigns in Grand Rapids, Mich., Des Moines, Iowa, Charlotte, N. C., Augusta, Ga., Altoona, Pa., Miami, Fla., and many other places. Thousands of converts in those places will be thankful through eternity for what happened when Billy Graham and his co-workers came to their cities.

But, somehow, in the autumn of 1949, things "just bubbled over."

When the campaign was completed, the report given by executive secretary C. C. Jenkins showed that 3000 people had professed Christ as personal Saviour. Another 3000 people either had re-consecrated their lives to Christ or come back to Christ weeping forgiveness for their sins. A total of 350,000 people had filed in and out of the mammoth tent in the 72 meetings. Times without number there were thousands of people standing along the outside. One crowd was estimated at more than 15,000 people, with 6000 of them standing on the outside.

Nothing unusual in the way of evangelism or revival happened in the first three scheduled weeks. Hundreds of people found Christ as Saviour, but this had been true in other places as well where the team had ministered or in previous Christ for Greater Los Angeles campaigns. But along toward the end of

the third week, the committee together with Graham felt that
something was beginning to stir. Still, it was hard to know
what to do. The plans called for stopping the campaign after
the final meeting on Sunday night, October 16.

Then one of the most important committee meetings in
modern-day evangelical history was held. The question: to continue or stop the meetings. After much, much prayer, the
decision was reached: Continue.

On the night of October 16, into the tent walked a man well
known throughout Los Angeles and Hollywood. For 21 years
he had been on the radio in the area. At the time he was conducting a program an hour and fifteen minutes each day on
KFWB in Hollywood. His horses had won as much as $50,000
in a single race at nearby Santa Anita race track. He was in
any man's language a "man's man." He had mentioned on his
program the campaign going on at Washington and Hill streets.
He even sat in on a few of the meetings at the insistence of
his praying wife.

His name: Stuart Hamblen.

Billy Graham said after the campaign was over, "If I could
have picked two men in Los Angeles whom I would have
liked to see converted in the campaign there, one of them would
have been Stuart Hamblen." He realized in even the short while
he was in Los Angeles that Hamblen was a key man in the
area, with tremendous influence.

The night that the campaign was scheduled to close, Hamblen
was in the tent. He had come home from a weekend hunting
trip which had not turned out too well. As he explained later,
he thought that if he could hold out for one more meeting
against the conviction surging in his own heart, he would be
all right.

When the committee announced that the campaign was to
continue another week, his heart sank. He was angry as he
walked from the tent that night. He explained later that he
did not know how long he could hold out.

In another chapter are the details leading up to the conversion of Stuart Hamblen on Monday morning, October 17, 1949, at 4:30 in the morning in Billy Graham's room in the Langham hotel in Los Angeles. We could not do justice, either, to the way in which this tremendously interesting individual has of telling it. But, it happened. God did a thorough job of it. Stuart Hamblen was born again through the power of the Holy Spirit.

That decision electrified the entire area.

The warmth of the testimony of a newly born-again Christian was heard the following day on a radio program. It startled thousands of listeners. It amazed them. It was a subject of ridicule and scorn by some all along Sunset Strip in Hollywood, a mile-long stretch of boulevard owned and frequented almost entirely by movie people. The odds there were 100 to 1 that he would not hold out a week. Then they slipped to 50 to 1, to 10 to 1. Finally you could not even get even money.

He sold his racing stable except for El Lobo, the favorite which he kept for sentimental reasons. The night that he gave his testimony of what Christ had done for him the tent was packed. Graham did not have to preach. He merely gave the invitation. Two weeks later there was hardly a dry eye in the great tent when Hamblen's aging mother and father from Abilene, Texas, mounted the platform and told of how God had answered prayer in behalf of their wayward son. Stuart Hamblen's father is a preacher of the gospel in the Methodist church.

The newspapers took immediate note. Entire pages were turned over to the campaign as editors realized that something newsworthy was going on. Pictures were taken by the hundred. Magazines sent crack reporters to get articles on Graham and the team. Three thousand seats were added to the tent, making seating capacity 9000. Yet there was not enough room, other thousands stood or were turned away. Then came the

Associated Press, United Press and International News Service dispatches spreading the campaign to every spot in America and Canada. *Life* and *Time* added to it, as well as many others.

Other leading people in Hollywood and Los Angeles were reached for Christ. Television actor Harvey Fritz, a man who only a year before had lined his family up against a wall in an adobe home in Arizona and threatened to kill them all, came to the tent one night. Only the courage of a 13-year old son who had stepped in front of Fritz' divorced wife and said, "Don't kill my mommy," had kept him from being a murderer. He was, in his own words, "a mean man." His program, "Out Wickenberg Way," heard regularly on KFI-TV, in Los Angeles, was one of the favorites in the region. People may have thought he was a good man, but he knew differently.

Conviction hit him so hard at the tent and in the prayer room following the message by Billy that he became belligerent. He tossed chairs around. No one was going to convert him! In anger he even tried to strike Clifford Smith, chairman of the committee. But near midnight that evening, God won another important victory. When Harvey Fritz opened his next television program he opened it with "Sweet Hour of Prayer" and "Shall We Gather at the River." He explained to his audience that they were more than words to a mere song. He also told of what God had done for him.

When the program was over, his sponsors told him not to mention the name of Jesus Christ on his programs again. To which a now-gentle but born-again Fritz could only say, "Jesus Christ means more to me than all of the radio programs in Hollywood." The contract was cancelled. He was a man without a job. But . . . he had Christ. Within a week he had visited his estranged wife in Arizona and left the children with not a fear for their daddy but a Gospel of John and a way to say grace at the table!

A faithful neighbor told Louis Zamperini, Olympic miler in 1936 and survivor of 47 days on a life raft in the recent war, of the meetings. Zamperini finally attended with his wife. They came back again, and again. On the third night, they went into the prayer tent and accepted Christ as Saviour.

As the press carried the reports of the campaign in increasing quantity, people in underworld as well as other walks of life took notice. Curiosity drew Jim Vaus, a friend of Mickey Cohen, to the tent one night. In Vaus' pocket was a ticket East to start a new job and make a tremendous amount of money as a wire tapper. But God had an eternal ticket ready for him. That night in the prayer tent, Jim Vaus took Christ as his personal Saviour. The plane ticket was ripped into bits. A new life was started. To the district attorney's office he went to make false testimony correct. Around the city he traveled to various people to make restitution. Opportunities unlimited opened to him to talk to his former friends of what Christ had done for Him. Again, the city sat up and took notice.

These are but four of the thousands who came to Christ. There is no doubt but that the turning to Christ of these four men and others equally as prominent did much to reach many unconverted people in the Los Angeles area. But, and here again it was made clear, it was no more important that they were converted than any of the other 3000 who came.

Graham wrote in an article in the January, 1950, *Youth for Christ Magazine,* that to him the success of the campaign was rooted in three things. First, the prayers of God's people. Secondly, the power of the Holy Spirit. Thirdly, the power of the Word of God.

Prayer meetings in behalf of the campaign had been started a full 18 months before even one service was held! Nine months before the opening night, they had begun to meet regularly. They kept it up steadily for the next nine months, with very few breaks. Several all-day prayer meetings had been held. During the campaign, a number of all-night prayer meetings were conducted. As Billy explained to the religious press after it was over, "Anyone could preach with that prayer support."

Wires and cables from all parts of the world reached the team, signifying that the senders were praying. Northwestern Schools in Minneapolis took an entire day off from classes to remember their leader. Prayer meetings at the evening services started 30 minutes prior to the opening song. Many times there was standing room only in the prayer tent! Cliff Smith very often had time only to read a fraction of the prayer requests which stacked high in his hand at that vital service.

No one but the men closest to the work of Christ for Greater Los Angeles committee will appreciate, either, of the definite answer to prayer which came only a few weeks before the campaign opened. That concerned where the tent was to be erected. Location after location had closed up. The committee was in human desperation before God. Suddenly the lot at Washington and Hill streets opened up, a corner to become sacred to thousands.

So deep was the moving of the Holy Spirit that at times Graham did not have to preach. After some of the testimonies from the converts all he had to do was give the invitation. And the sinners came, seeking Christ. One night of the final week he was half way through his message when a man ran down the aisle, called up to Graham on the platform and asked if he could become a Christian right then. Billy referred him to T. W. Wilson, assistant president at Northwestern Schools, who then was helping him, and they went into the prayer tent. When Billy stood up again to get back into his sermon, he was prompted by the Holy Spirit to give the invitation right then. He did, and about 200 people went into the prayer tent.

All possible hindrances to the working of the Holy Spirit were removed during the campaign. Applause was kept at a bare minimum. There was little instrumental music or singing of choruses. Beverly Shea concentrated on the old gospel songs which had been used of God so greatly in the past. Cliff Barrows centered his song leading and programming around the hymns of revival of days past, using as a theme song, "Send a Great Revival in My Soul."

Skeptics who came to find fault with Graham's messages went away with but one conclusion. They could not argue with Graham. Their argument was with the Word of God.

Those huge crowds were told a number of times each night, it seemed, that "This isn't Billy Graham's opinion. This is the Word of God." The sermons he gave were peppered and sprinkled freely with the Word of God. Illustrations went out the window. Graham merely declared the Word of God and hungry people responded. As the campaign continued he would spend from six to eight hours a day in working out new messages, secluding himself from everyone in order to get alone with God and receive the message He had for him to give to people.

The prayer tent was a separate canvas building right alongside the main tent. Entrances to it were from both sides of the platform. As these who responded to the invitation reached the smaller tent, they were met by I. A. "Daddy" Moon at one entrance or Ben Weiss at the other. These two men were in a large way responsible for the follow-up work and the personal counselling in the prayer tent. The experiences they can tell and have told could form a book in themselves. On at least two instances, divorced couples met in the prayer tent, were re-united after making decisions to accept Christ, and made immediate plans to be remarried. Entire families were converted. One personal worker led 92 people to Christ during the eight weeks. Two pastors of the city came to know Christ as Saviour. A member of the vice squad of the Los Angeles police department was saved. And so many more, each with a separate story of God's power to cleanse and save from sin.

In the background of it was the Christ for Greater Los Angeles committee headed by Smith and Jenkins. They had done in a human way all that could be done to prepare the way for revival. J. Edwin Orr, well known around the world for his

keen interest in revival, was sent through the area for an entire month prior to the campaign, speaking and creating prayer
interest. Armin Gesswein of Pasadena, veteran of the Norway
revivals of the 1940's, spent two weeks doing the same thing.
Grady Wilson, Billy's associate evangelist, came two weeks early.
Graham and Barrows came a week prior to the campaign to
meet the committees for prayer and check final details. (It was
during that week that Graham made his first contact with
Stuart Hamblen.) Everything was done to make the 480-foot
long tent as comfortable and as attractively decorated as possible.
Everyone agreed when it was over that "This was of God," but
a mountain of human effort and work also had gone into it.

Through it all, moved the men of the team with an easy
and confident step that God was working. Cliff Barrows was
in charge of the music from beginning to end, as well as the
conducting of the meeting. The 26-year old graduate of Bob
Jones University and his wife, Billie, at one of the organs made
a perfect musical team. Experience on both sides of the Atlantic
and in thousands of Youth for Christ and other meetings had
prepared them for this challenge.

Beverly Shea, son of a Methodist pastor, brought the songs
of the gospel to the throngs in a quiet, reverent way. His solo
immediately preceding Graham's message was of special depth
as it prepared the hearts of the listeners for the sermon. As
Graham once said, in starting to speak, "We might even give
the invitation right now."

Associate Evangelist Grady Wilson spent the first three weeks
of the campaign there, then had to leave for another campaign
at which he was scheduled. Thus he did not get to see God
working in the amazing way which developed. Wilson is a
native of Charlotte, N. C., and grew up along with Billy in
that city. On his shoulders fell much of the detail of the team
as well as the carrying on in the preaching on a number of
occasions.

In this day of wondering what makes atomic energy develop and explode and all of the discussion on the hydrogen bomb, other people are wondering as they look at Billy Graham and see the tremendous job he is doing, "What keeps Billy ticking?"

What is it that has brought this lank, handsome southern lad to the place where people are tagging him as the next great revivalist?

What has been the molding process of this unusual young man of God as he has developed into an international figure?

Billy was born in Charlotte, N. C., the son of Frank and Morrow Graham, on November 7, 1918. His father was a dairy farmer. The family was Southern Presbyterian and it was in that church that Billy grew up. He developed into a sports-loving young fellow who loved baseball above the rest of them. First base was his specialty and he played it well.

One day in 1936, evangelist Mordecai Ham came to Charlotte to hold a campaign. Billy scoffed inwardly at the efforts he made at winning people to Christ, but one night the lanky first baseman was in attendance at the tent. When the invitation was given, 16-year old Billy walked down the sawdust aisle to accept Christ as his Saviour.

He felt an urge to preach almost immediately, and did a lot of it in the missions and churches around home as he finished high school. Then he enrolled at the Florida Bible Institute in Tampa, Florida, for Bible training. When he had completed his training there he went to Bob Jones University (then at Cleveland, Tenn.) for a term or two before transferring to Wheaton College in Wheaton, Illinois, where he completed his college work. It was at Wheaton that he met the daughter of a returned Southern Presbyterian medical missionary to China, Ruth Bell. Things progressed in the normal romantic way and they were married on Friday, August 13, 1943, at Montreat, N. C. Into their home at Montreat, a few miles from Charlotte, have come two girls, Virginia, 4, and Ann, 2. Reporters once asked

Mrs. Graham how she liked it with Billy being away from home so much. She told them, "I'd rather spend a little time with him than a lot of time with any other man in the whole world." Her heart is solidly behind the work being carried on by her husband no matter what the sacrifice she may be called on to make.

While at Wheaton, Graham pastored the Village Church of Western Springs, a few miles from Wheaton. When he finished school, he accepted a call to be a full-time pastor there. Included in his church schedule was a Sunday evening radio program of 45 minutes duration which brought his ministry into the homes of thousands in the Chicago area. The program, "Songs in the Night," had Beverly Shea and the King's Karrollers as the main musical basis with Graham interspersing brief comments between the musical numbers. The program soon became one of the most popular in the region.

One day in January, 1945, Dr. Torrey M. Johnson of Chicago, then the pastor of the Midwest Bible church, director of Chicagoland Youth for Christ and beginning to assume the responsibilities of Youth for Christ International in its formative stages, called Billy Graham on the phone and invited him to come to Chicago to talk about Youth for Christ. The two men met in a barren office room at 130 N. Wells Street in Chicago, and after a long prayer session, Johnson asked Graham to become the first paid employee of Youth for Christ International. Billy was led of God to accept it.

Then followed three years of the most strenuous evangelistic campaigning that he ever has gone through. Billy reached all parts of the United States and Canada in speaking at Youth for Christ rallies and conferences as the movement mushroomed in all parts of the continent. He spared himself not a bit as he moved through the swirl of the beginning of this movement which now has rallies in 59 countries of the world.

Only eternity will reveal the tremendous amount of work done through Graham in working with Torrey Johnson, Charles

Templeton, Dick Harvey, Bob Cook and others in those early days of Youth for Christ. He was one of five men—Johnson, Graham, Templeton, Stratton Shufelt and newspaperman Wesley Hartzell—who made that important Youth for Christ European survey trip in the spring of 1946. In the fall of 1946 he left America together with Cliff and Billie Barrows to spend six months in England as a Youth for Christ team. That was one of England's coldest winters because of the low temperatures and the lack of fuel. By March, 1947, however the campaigns had been so successful that a national Youth for Christ conference called in Birmingham resulted in the formation of British Youth for Christ. Thousands of people were won to Christ in those six months of campaign. British Youth for Christ then was left with the challenge to carry on the work.

On four other occasions Graham has been to Europe since the end of the war. His ministry has been felt in almost every country of Europe, both through messages delivered in those places or through contact with the many delegates at the Youth for Christ World Congress on Evangelism at Beatenberg, Switzerland, in August, 1948.

Anyone watching him at work in those days might well have said even as they say now when he is in the midst of a revival campaign, "How can he stand up under it?"

It has been only through strength given to him by God that he has been able to stand the pace. He was a sick man after the six months spent in England. As one reporter wrote in one story, "Graham looks and feels like a dishrag, after a message." But a burning passion and zeal to win men to Christ forces him to go on.

On December 7, 1948, he accepted the presidency of Northwestern Schools in Minneapolis, Minnesota, the school founded and directed for so many years by Dr. W. B. Riley. On his sick bed a number of months before he died, Dr. Riley had designated Billy Graham as his successor. Graham turned the offer down at first, but later accepted it. He is able to spend about 20 per cent of his time in Minneapolis and has gathered around him a capable teaching faculty which is doing a thorough job in Christian education in the Bible school, seminary and college departments. In the 1949-50 school year there were 1150 students in day school from 41 states and 17 foreign countries. In traveling in Europe, Graham saw the need of trained personnel in those countries and has instigated at Northwestern a policy whereby foreign students need pay no tuition or board or room.

At about the same time that he assumed the presidency of Northwestern Schools he formed the evangelistic team which in a unique way has been used of God to bring revival fires burning in many sections of our land. Barrows was a natural choice for the songleader. Methodist-backgrounded Beverly Shea, who said once, "I was brought up with the smell of Methodist camp meetings in my nostrils," came along as the soloist. It meant it would keep him away from some of the meetings because of his having to return to Chicago each Tuesday morning for his network broadcast, but Shea was willing to do that.

So they started, with their first campaign in Grand Rapids, Mich.; Des Moines, Iowa, was next, followed by Augusta, Ga., then Miami, Fla., Altoona, Pa., and others. In each place the Lord blessed their efforts and many converts were won to a personal faith in Christ. Day in and day out they came to know each other in a better way and to mold their three personalities into a workable revival unit. Mrs. Billie Barrows accompanied at the organ or the piano. Grady Wilson, boyhood chum of Billy's, rounded out the team in the roll of associate evangelist.

Campaign after campaign proved to be the "biggest held in our city for many years." The ripples of revival were not felt in those cases, but the Holy Spirit did eternal work in hundreds of lives in each city.

Billy's preaching style remained the same. His command of the platform increased with each series. As one of the top orators in evangelical Christianity he attracted people to hear him just to study how he spoke. Many remained to be converted. Up and down the platform he strode, his arms raised or lowered as the case might be, his eyes burning out the message on his heart. Photographers by the scores watched him catlike as he delivered his messages. Veteran preachers were warmed in a strange way as he held aloft his Bible and quoted freely from the Word of God as he spoke.

In Los Angeles he used for the first time the lapel microphone which allowed him freedom of action as he spoke. Keeping the attention of that vast throng in Los Angeles was a task in itself. A portion of the people sat in front of him, looking at him straight on. Another great section would have had to look at one side of his face had he preached straight ahead all of the time. The other great section would have seen the other side of his face. So he walked back and forth—five long strides each way—sometimes stopping halfway across and coming back toward one side. Sitting behind him to see that the lapel cord did not trip him up was his buddy Cliff Barrows.

There was no holding back in his preaching. Every ounce of his energy was poured into the message. His voice gave out in all of its strength and power as he declared the power of God and the salvation of people through belief in Christ's death for them on the cross. His messages were fresh each night. Some of them may have been given before, but they were delivered from a warm heart which was thumping with the challenge of lost and dying people sitting before him.

The Bible would be laid on the pulpit to give him more freedom. He would stop, place his hands on his knees and drive home another point in all its sincerity and power.

When invitation time came, he again was in command. There was no sugary-voiced pleading for people to come to Christ. It was a man-to-man approach. The invitations were not prolonged after people had stopped coming. When he felt that God had completed His work in a service, he would close the meeting. After a brief time of shaking hands with friends, back to the prayer tent he would go for personal counselling of the converts. This was a vital part of his night of ministry as he told them of things which would help them in their Christian living.

Then back to his room after stopping in some off-the-path eating place for a little food refreshment. Once in his room he would relax and review the day's activities, especially the night's service. Many a time sleep would not be his for hours as his body and mind recuperated from the efforts of the evening. But, when sleep did come, he would sleep the rest of the faithful servant of Christ whose life is centered in Him.

During the day, and while at home, he reads much to keep abreast of the times. His messages are up-to-date. He is right to the minute on what is happening around the world. He eats healthy normal meals, though the time he eats varies with his preaching schedules. At times when his mind is tied in with the message to come, you may see him just sitting and pecking away at the food.

Space does not permit here a well-detailed picture of the man whom Oswald J. Smith has described as "America's next great revivalist." When you see him you'll find him well dressed. His ties are bright, his clothes found in the young business men's and youth's department of a store. Wide-brimmed hats are a favorite. Flaming argyle socks are the rule, not the exception.

If two words could describe him, they would be "sincerity and humility." Any time people tend to praise him for anything, he says, "This has been God's doing. He deserves *ALL* the praise."

And he means it.

His heart is soft, he has a kind word for anyone he meets. If time permits, he will speak to anyone he sees. If not, he will be pleasant in excusing himself.

When he returned from Los Angeles to Minneapolis after the campaign there, he slipped into the city the night before to avoid a student welcome home for him at the depot. That noon he talked to the Northwestern faculty and a few pastors at a luncheon in the Curtis hotel in Minneapolis. He was a a subdued man as he spoke, subdued in the sense that God had watered him down to a usable size in the previous eight weeks. He reported on the meetings, gave a few personal opinions of how God was working and the reasons he had for the success of the meetings.

In the closing words, the great heart of Billy Graham bared itself wide open. He could not thank the faculty members enough for their prayers in his behalf. When he came to mention the lengthy telegram they had sent him when the decision was made to continue the seventh week and thus necessitate his staying away from the school's annual founder's week, in which the closing words were, "We love you, Billy," he broke down. Tears filled his eyes, he chocked up, said a few more words, and sat down.

So we have seen a glimpse of Billy Graham, man of God for the mid-century.

CONTINUING REVIVAL—*at Boston*

BOSTON is some 3000 miles from Los Angeles. But when Billy Graham, Cliff Barrows, Beverly Shea and Grady Wilson arrived in Boston on December 30, 1949, for a nine-day campaign at the Park Street Church pastored by Dr. Harold John Ockenga, they found that the same warm moving of the Holy Spirit in which the Los Angeles meetings had ended was present in Boston.

So prevalent was it that they started the campaign a day early, with some 2000 people present in the Park Street Church on December 30. The next night, when it officially opened, more than 6000 people packed into the Mechanics building on New Year's Eve, the world's worst night for evangelism. On a moment's notice the hall was rented for the next afternoon—New Year's day. Another filled house was the result. That night in the Park Street Church, more than 2500 attended.

Boston newspapers gave the meetings front page space. They continued to do so for the next 18 days as the campaign moved from Mechanics building to the Park Street Church to the Opera house, back to Mechanics building and finally to the Boston Garden on Monday, January 16.

Fill the Boston Garden for a revival meeting in a city 74 per cent Catholic and 15 per cent Unitarian? Impossible, you might say.

But, GOD DID IT AGAIN.

The Boston Garden seats 14,000 people. When 16,000 had flocked into that mammoth indoor arena, fire officials closed the doors. Ten thousand people were turned away. Twenty five hundred stayed in the lobbies to hear the meeting through loud speakers. Cliff Barrows led a choir of 2500 voices in many wonderful hymns. Mrs. Graham came from Montreat, N. C., to give a testimony. The crowd was thrilled when Dr. Ockenga announced that although the campaign was stopping that night for lack of a suitable place to meet that it would be continued late in March and into April in towns throughout New England and in Boston.

Graham spoke on Noah and the ark. Never, it seemed, was he better than this night. His green tie slightly loosened, his eyes flashing with sincerity, he roamed a wide circle around the pulpit as he brought to that great crowd the facts of sin, righteousness and judgment to come.

When he was through, he asked no one to leave while he gave the invitation. As he asked for those who wished to accept Christ to raise their hands, people all over the main floor arena and into the second and third balconies put up their hands. It seemed as though hands shot up from all parts of the place almost at once. When he asked everyone to stand and the converts to come to the front of the platform, they came in an unending stream. Usually he would ask them to wait there for a moment while he dismissed the audience with a word of prayer. But on this night, which New England was not soon to forget, so many people came that he had to send them right on into the prayer rooms reserved for personal counselling.

Finally, word came from the prayer room which seated 1000 people that there was no more room there. The remainder were asked to stand in front of the platform. They filled it solidly on three sides and back up the aisles in the main floor. Graham asked the audience to sit down as he spoke to the converts and personal workers and pastors handed out copies of the Gospel of John and secured the decision cards. When the meeting was dismissed and the people had made their way home, more than 1500 people had professed faith in Jesus Christ!

In one single meeting!

Boston and New England quivered with revival. Newspapers the following morning gave extensive front page reporting and photographic coverage. In all three morning papers it was

the main story on page one. *The Boston Post* ran 10 pictures
and two complete inside pages of campaign highlights. Graham's
message was reported almost in full.

How had it happened?

Once again, prayer. The Park Street Church had prayed
for a year and a half for the campaign. Day-long prayer sessions spotlighted the campaign. Preachers met at different times
to pray. When it was over, more than 75 churches in the area
were co-operating.

Once again, it was a demonstration of faith to believe God
that things would happen. Money had been needed to get it
started. It was forthcoming from members of the Park Street
Church. Money was needed to get the Boston Garden. It was
forthcoming. The skeptics said, "Boston Garden? Brother, take
it easy." They added, "Start a campaign on New Year's Eve?
Never been done before. Belongs to the devil."

One eye-witness to the last four days of the Boston campaign
was Robert C. Van Kampen, of Van Kampen Press. His testimony of what he saw there is thrilling:

"We have often wondered what it was like when Peter
spoke at Pentecost as Acts 2:41 tells us: 'Then they gladly received his word and were baptized, and the same day there
were added unto them about three thousand souls.' What a
marvelous and thrilling experience! Of course, that could only
happen in early church history! We have read of the Finney,
Moody and Sunday Revivals and have said in our own hearts:
'It can't happen now—we are too sophisticated, too hard-boiled
and too well educated,' but we did see it happen in Boston
in January.

"Friday night we saw close to 400 come forward, Saturday
night another large group. On Sunday afternoon several thousand people could not get into Mechanics hall that was already
packed with 8,000 people. Over forty people in the street raised
their hands for salvation. Then came Monday night. The
meeting was moved to Boston Garden, holding 16,000 people.

Some critics had doubted that there would be sufficient people to fill the main auditorium, but at seven o'clock the gates were locked and thousands were left in the streets outside. When the invitation was given, people came forward in droves, quietly—some crying—others just looking serious. As one *Boston Globe* reporter stated: 'Among those many hundreds, there was no seeming hysteria. Those who cried looked as if they shed tears of relief or happiness. Others walked forward quietly, serenely, as if they knew a long time ahead that they were ready to look for the better life that Graham told them Christ offered.'

"They came all ages, colors and creeds. A young Chinese boy at the age where boys seldom cry was weeping unashamedly. Men of wealth and position, along with those who were down and out, stood side by side in front of the great platform confessing that they had accepted Christ as their personal Saviour.

"I will never forget Friday night. A young man about twenty-five years old came forward along with several hundred others. A woman, apparently in her fifties, came forward also and they literally fell in each other's arms, both weeping. The young man said: 'Mother, will you forgive me?' The woman said: 'John, will you ever forgive me?' The two had been separated for years, and were now reunited—neither knowing that the other was at the meeting that the other was accepting Christ when the invitation was given.

"The amazing thing to me was the dignity in which all of the meetings were conducted. There was little applause at the end of a solo or choir number, for Cliff Barrows requested that if you approve, say, ' "Amen," in your own heart.'

"God has blessed Billy Graham with remarkable speaking ability, and a deep insight to His Word. Billy did not give any deep messages. He presented the simple gospel without illustration or story. The emphasis of his sermon was always the same—'God has said,' 'the Bible tells us,' 'God has promised,' and he constantly quoted Scripture. As Peter of old said: 'Repent, and be baptized every one of you in the name of Jesus Christ for the remission of sins,' so Billy talked of sin and the necessity of repentance and being born again. It was not the doings of any person, and again in the words of the evangelist: 'It isn't the doings of Billy Graham; it is a miracle that God, Himself, has brought to New England in 1950.'

"While riding with us to the auditorium on Friday night, one of the reporters who was covering the campaign, turned and said, 'If Billy stays here another week, he will have every one of the reporters converted. We don't understand what we see. It doesn't make sense. We can't understand why the newspapers are behind him, but we are seeing something that Boston hasn't seen as long as I have been a reporter in the City.' He told us that more people turned out to the Billy Graham meeting at the Gardens than ever turned out to see a President of the United States.

"Proof that this was not a one-man campaign but a working of the Holy Spirit is seen in the fact that pastors all over the Boston area reported improved church attendance and conversions. One pastor, who had attended many of the meetings, admitted that in two years he had not had a single conversion in his church. Billy told him that he had to preach the simple gospel and get back to old-fashioned Bible exposition. He promised he would. Sunday noon, while we were having lunch, he called excitedly at the hotel to report that that morning he had forty-five converts.

"Another pastor had put in his resignation January 1 because he told his church: 'I have been here three years and haven't seen any results from my ministry.' Several of his young people were saved in one of Billy's meetings . . . others were saved, and on Sunday morning, two weeks after he had put in his resignation, he announced to the church: 'I am withdrawing my resignation. We have twenty-seven converts in our own church as the result of this revival and I am going to stay and feed my babes.'

"Many stories could be told of complete families that were converted, of interesting sidelights, but the thing that is most important is that there is a definite moving of the Holy Spirit in New England—such as has not been in evidence for thirty or forty years. Let us all pray that God will continue this revival, not only in New England, but throughout the United States, and that nothing will be done by any of His servants to hinder this great work."

The summary showed that at least 3000 people professed Christ in the 18 days of services. More than 105,000 people attended the meetings. Thus God did in 18 days what He had taken eight weeks to do in Los Angeles. He had done it without a single piece of decoration in any of the buildings in which the services were held.

He had taken a one-church campaign and fanned it throughout six New England states. He had taken the faith of such men as Dr. Ockenga, Allan Emery, Jr., chairman, Fred Lincoln, head of counsellors, Gordon Sanders, publicity man, and flamed it into something that "ABSOLUTELY COULD NOT HAPPEN IN BOSTON!"

The fires are still ablaze as this is being written.

God did it again.

He will do it again.

PREPARING FOR THE REVIVAL

by J. Edwin Orr

"THIS is holy ground," said Billy Graham. We were standing in the little bedroom in Lincoln College where John Wesley and his fellow-students had begun the Holy Club, and on the wall was a picture showing the Wesleys, Whitefield, and others in session.

That day was spent in visiting Oxford University's halls of learning, but the North Carolinian evangelist did not only want to see the sights, but to talk about the hope and prospect of another great evangelical awakening such as Wesley experienced.

A couple of years later in his office in the Northwestern Schools in Minneapolis, we were together with two young Californians, Dunlap and Franck. It was close to one in the morning, but we knelt and prayed. The previous October, 1948, Armin Gesswein and I had shared a prayer conference with sixty Minneapolis ministers, and there was outpoured a spirit of confession and consecration which transformed many a life. Three months later, the same group of ministers experienced another stirring of the Spirit at Camp Iduhapi, where we shared with them a vision of revival in the Christian colleges of the Twin Cities. "God grant it," said Billy Graham in that prayer meeting in April.

Within a week, a student revival described by President Wingblade as "unprecedented" had broken forth at Bethel College across the Mississippi in St. Paul, all science, arts and theology classes being abandoned in favor of prayer, confession, restitution and decision. Reviving in varied degree was felt in half dozen other colleges, and more than two thousand students testified of personal reviving, restoration or regeneration through the Spirit's impact. The United Spiritual Advance movement—

in a report furnished by Paul Rees, Victor Nelson, and Wallace Mikkelson, co-chairman of the ministerial fellowship—pointed out that "equally amazing is the fact that Christians . . . have agreed unanimously that the student campaign has been an outpouring of the Spirit from start to finish. The Lord alone knows what will follow this work of preparation."

Billy Graham was in Los Angeles preparing for his fall campaign when Dr. Wingblade telephoned him to announce the outpouring of the Spirit at Bethel. Seven weeks earlier, we had flown from Montreal to Los Angeles to engage in a month of meetings calculated to deepen the spiritual life of Christians in Los Angeles in preparation for the Billy Graham campaign. The series was under the auspices of the same Christ for Greater Los Angeles committee planning the Graham effort, and they kept us busy in sixty or more meetings in churches and other groups.

By far the most outstanding gathering was the Ministers' Conference for prayer for revival organized by Armin Gesswein at Pacific Palisades Conference Grounds. Several hundred ministers, evangelists, missionaries, and their wives, shared in another extraordinary outpouring of the Spirit, and the evening sessions continued until long after midnight. Pastors from historic and traditional Protestant denominations participated freely with pastors from the younger denominations and independent groups.

There was confession and restitution of a striking nature, but the details were forgotten as the Heavenly Father pulled the curtain of forgiveness across the place. There was blessing also in ministerial, congregational, and organizational meetings throughout greater Los Angeles. The Lord blessed the Word, and many were convinced that, as was said by Matthew Henry, "when God intends great mercy for His people, He first of all sets them a-praying."

Just as Armin Gesswein's work among ministers culminated in an outpouring of the Spirit in 1949, so Henrietta Mears' work among students had the same effect. Two years previously, there had been a flash flood of unusual blessing at a student conference at the beautiful Forest Home Conference Grounds a mile high in the San Bernardino Mountains. The 1947 movement was so sudden and unexpected that not all its results were conserved, but it made all participants thirsty for another revival. So, in 1949, the Young Adult Conference in July was greatly owned of God, not the least of the fruitage being the surrender of a young radio star who immediately became burdened for the spiritually needy stars in the world of radio, television, stage, and screen. A direct outcome was a weekly gathering of a group of famous people in Beverly Hills. This group soon became self-governing, the direction gladly being turned over to the stars themselves.

Blessed as was the July Conference, it was nothing compared to the September Student Briefing Conference at Forest Home. No less than 500 students from a dozen universities and many colleges attended. The ministry was shared by a team of leaders, David Cowie, "Dad" Elliott, Louis Evans, Bob Ferguson, Dick Halverson, Bob Munger, Miss Mears, Billy Graham and myself. Billy Graham brought inspirational messages in the morning meetings at 11; in the evening meetings we had the privilege of giving doctrinal and challenging messages. The topics were, in sequence: God and Students; Revival, the Work of God; How God Forgives Sins; the Searchlight of God; Sanctification, Imputed, Critical and Progressive; the Filling of the Spirit; the Impact of Revival.

There was blessing in all the meetings, but the climax was reached on the Wednesday evening when the meeting continued in power until midnight. Much confession was made, but all of it under the restraint of the Spirit, with not a regrettable utterance. Reviving of believers, restoration of backsliders, regeneration of sinners proceeded in such a remarkable way that the veteran student evangelist, "Dad" Elliott, declared that it was the most unusual meeting of his experience since the glorious days of the Student Volunteers last century.

The overflow from this conference had its effect on many a campus on the Pacific Coast, and even provoked a revival in a church in far-away Colorado. Enthusiasm was boundless, and yet there was no emotionalism, the order of the Spirit's impact seeming to be first intellectual, then volitional, then emotional; tears sometimes following conviction, and joy following the cleansing of sin. Perhaps the most significant thing was the emphasis that the confession of sin and consequent cleansing were only preparatory to appropriating by faith a sanctified and Spirit-filled life. For many it meant abandoning a life on a lower plane, with occasional excursions to higher levels by balloon, for living on a plateau of higher Christian life, feet planted on the solid ground of the promises of God.

Undoubtedly the direct instrument under God in the bringing of Billy Graham to Los Angeles and the sustaining organization in the success of the meetings was the Christ for Greater Los Angeles committee. Cliff Smith and Claude Jenkins and many another leader in the committee had been stirred by the Pacific Palisades Conference in March, and were tiptoe in expectancy of real revival. The committee worked together in the campaign most harmoniously, and once the movement was under way the committee was possessed by a holy enthusiasm. The Christ for Greater Los Angeles Committee drew its main support from the National Association of Evangelicals constituency, but there were others from affiliations to the right and left of the NAE position helping loyally without giving up their opinions on co-operation. The officers of the Christ for Greater Los Angeles committee were deeply spiritual men, a sort of advance guard in the reviving.

The story of the Los Angeles Big Tent Campaign is now well-known. For eight weeks, in the last quarter of the year, an unseasonable heat-wave persisted with the daily temperatures hovering in the eighties. November was warmer than June. At a critical point, a Pacific storm threatened to break up the fine weather spell, but following a prayer meeting, the storm moved out to sea again and missed the city. Without this extraordinary weather, the Big Tent Campaign would have been handicapped. The Graham campaign was followed by the worst fogs of Los Angeles history, dislocating traffic for weeks.

The Big Tent seated six thousand, and soon began to fill up. Night after night for the first two weeks, Billy Graham preached repentance to Christians. In the third week of October, a revival of the Bethel College pattern swept Northern Baptist Seminary in Chicago, where the chapel was crowded with students until midnight. The same week the Big Tent Campaign moved into high gear.

Some weeks previously, in the luxurious home of a well-known movie star, we had spent an hour with Stuart Hamblen, cowboy radio star, seeking to lead him to Christ. He was on the brink of dicision, but drowned his conviction in alcohol the following day. When Billy Graham came to the Stars' Group, he further impressed Stuart Hamblen. Hamblen's father was a minister, so Hamblen knew the way of salvation, although he carefully evaded the personal issue. But in the third week in October, when Northern students in Chicago were praying for Billy Graham in their morning watch, a father prayed most of the night for his unsaved son. A convicted Stuart Hamblen and his praying wife Susie left their Arcadia home sometime after four in the morning, drove west to Los Angeles to make decision at Billy Graham's hotel room.

Without doubt, the 1949 Big Tent Campaign was the greatest of its kind in Californian history. An aggregate of 400,000 people attended the eight weeks' meetings, and 4178 decision cards were turned in by the personal workers in the inquiry room. Of these, 2703 were first-time decisions. The Christ for Greater Los Angeles committee handled the distribution of the cards, sending cards to the pastor of any church specified, or to the nearest co-operating church of any denomination specified, or to the nearest co-operating evangelical church if no denomination were specified.

The success of the campaign quickened the hope of revival throughout America. Already, with the extraordinary revival of pastors in March, churches were reporting the doubling of prayer meetings and increased soul-winning up and down the Pacific Coast. The Graham campaign accelerated the movement, and the end is not yet.

SINGING DURING REVIVAL
by Cliff Barrows

Omitted

PRACTICALLY every great moving of the Spirit of God resulting in a spiritual awakening, has been accompanied by great singing. It was so in the days of the revival under the Wesleys. The revival of 1859 was a time of hymn singing. In the Moody and Sankey meetings gospel songs were fully half the power. Music played a prominent part in the great Welch revival with Evan Roberts.

And so it was in the Los Angeles and Boston campaigns. It would be hard to place one part of the service above another. Each had a very important place in the ministry of the Word. But I believe one of the most thrilling phases was the congregational singing. Some of the best singing was that which took place before the service actually began, as the people sat together thinking and praying. They just naturally burst into songs of praise and thanksgiving to God, such songs as "Shall We Gather At the River," and "There's a Land that is Fairer than Day."

In Los Angeles the people filled streetcars and buses both coming to the meetings and on the way home singing gospel choruses and especially the theme chorus we used for the campaign: "Send a Great Revival in My Soul." Often the conductor would join them. We never had a benediction at the close of our services, we always sang this chorus. It stirred the hearts of thousands of people as they visited the "canvas cathedral" night after night.

The special musical talent which helped during the Los Angeles campaign was greatly used of God to reach hearts. We had as soloist George Beverly Shea from Chicago, affectionately known as "Bev." He is heard coast to coast on the ABC network in a program of gospel hymns, called Club Time, and on "Songs in the Night" every Sunday evning over WENR, Chicago's ABC outlet. He is one of the most beloved gospel singers in America today, and certainly one who has won his way into the hearts of hundreds of thousands of people, not only in this country but in Great Britain as well, through his singing of the old gospel hymns and songs, and his own intrepretation of Negro sprituals.

Bev Shea usually sang from three to five numbers during an evening and many times at the close of his song, just before the message, an invitation could have been given, such was the spirit of conviction that had settled down upon the audience.

Another young man whose ministry in music and song was so highly effective was Charles Turner, second tenor of the Haven of Rest Quartet and a well-known voice not only in Los Angeles, but over the country where his music has been heard chiefly through recordings.

On Sundays frequently Jack Ranes, head of the department of music of the Pacific Bible College and director of music at the great Trinity Methodist Church in downtown Los Angeles, ably handled the congregational singing during the early part of the service.

Mrs. Kay Stewart and Mrs. Ellen Elsner, formerly known as the Collins Twins in the Los Angeles area, also brought real blessing to many as their blended voices stirred the hearts of thousands night after night. It was our privilege to hear Rev. Wilbur Nelson of the Huntington Park Grace Church, the Haven of Rest Quartet, the Old Fashioned Revival Hour Quartet, as well as Dr. Kerney Kegan, pastor of the great Temple Baptist Church in Los Angeles, during the campaign.

Our team for the first three weeks of the meeting included Mr. and Mrs. Wilmos Cshey of Alliance, Ohio. Mr. Cshey is a widely known concert violinist whose talent and ability has been dedicated solely to the Lord. His inimitable intrepretation of old gospel hymns and songs of the faith were a tremendous inspiration and blessing.

Mrs. Cshey was one of the skilled pianists of the campaign. Mrs. Elsie Dean Morphis took over as pianist following Mrs. Cshey. Mrs. Cliff Barrows held forth at the other piano.

Loren Whitney, well known in Los Angeles and throughout the Pacific Coast and nation as organist for the Haven of Rest broadcast, heard daily in the Los Angeles area and over a major network as well, presided at the organ. His sweet, humble spirit and willingness to do anything to be a blessing will never be forgotten.

I believe the ministry of music in a revival campaign should be different from that in a youth rally. In revival campaigns we have found that people love to sing the old gospel songs and hymns best. Even in young people's work, I have found this to be true. We do need the new choruses, we do need the new songs, for many of them express not only the joy of a wonderful new life in Christ, but also contain a real message for the heart and of blessing, when sung in the Spirit. But I believe we need to get back to the hymns and songs which will produce conviction in the heart of the unsaved and cause Christians to realize fully all the blessings that are theirs in Christ. This should be an inspiration and encouragement to contemporary hymn writers to express in their songs the great truths of God's word.

Song is a vital part of a spiritual revival. Those who came night after night at Los Angeles will long remember the spontaneous outbursts of old hymns, at the tent, on the streets and corners and in the cars, and buses, and the theme chorus:

> "Send a great revival in my soul.
> Send a great revival in my soul.
> Let the Holy Spirit come and take control.
> And send a great revival in my soul."

HARVESTING AT THE REVIVAL—
in Columbia

by Donald E. Hoke

HARVEST TIME for souls came to Columbia, South Carolina, in March, 1950, when God reaped over 7,000 decisions for Christ in what was probably the greatest evangelistic campaign in America in a generation. Climax of this great Billy Graham crusade came the final Sunday afternoon in a gigantic stadium rally where approximately 2000 persons filed onto the gridiron to confess Christ.

Cars from all the surrounding states began threading their way down South Carolina highways toward the great University of South Carolina football stadium on the final Sunday afternoon, March 12. At 11:00 a.m. the stands began to fill for the three o'clock rally. By 1:00 p.m. half of the 33,000 seats were filled. By 2:30 the grandstands overflowed down onto the north end of the gridiron, where revival-hungry people sat around on the grass. By the opening hour 40,000 people were packed into the huge stadium, and state troopers turned 10,000 more away.

It was a day of miracles from the outset. All week long weather forecasters predicted showers for Sunday. The morning papers carried a rain forecast on the front page. But Columbians had gathered in a downtown church all day Friday for prayer. Saturday night a 15-hour continuous prayer chain was begun.

And God heard! Sunday morning dawned warm and sunny. The temperature hovered over 70 degrees all day long as the sun smiled down from blue skies, broken only occasionally by fleecy clouds.

Quietly, intently, the huge crowd listened to introductions, applauded for Justice James Byrnes, former Secretary of State, when Evangelist Billy Graham introduced him, and shook the stands as Cliff Barrows led familiar old hymns.

The wind whisked Billy's hair about his face as he stood up to preach. "As it was in the days of Noah, so shall it be in the days when the Son of Man cometh," he read in the Word of God, pointing out that the prevalent sins of Noah's day have eaten out the moral heart of America today. He declared that Noah's message in the days before the flood is God's message to America—and Columbia—today! "Repent and turn to God."

Led to cut his message short, Dr. Graham prayed, asked for hands of those who wanted to trust Christ as Saviour. Then as the audience sang solemnly "Just as I am, without one plea," scores and hundreds began to file quietly out of the vast horse-shoe stadium onto the gridiron in front of the rostrum until almost 2,000 stood with heads bowed.

"This has been the greatest single meeting in which I've ever been," Billy Graham said. "I've never spoken to such a large crowd before, and I've never seen God work like this in America or Europe."

A great day of harvest had come to South Carolina. Governor J. Strom Thurmond said that never in the history of the state has so great a crowd been gathered for any event. And local ministers were universal in their praise of the closing meeting and the whole campaign in a front-page newspaper article the following day.

That Columbia was the scene of the greatest harvest of souls for Christ in America in a generation, there can be little doubt. Early in the campaign Dr. Graham and his party sensed that Columbia was uniquely ripe as no city had been in their experience. Repeatedly he cried to the ministers of the city, "Put ye in the sickle, for the harvest is ripe!" (Joel 3:3) And as Billy Graham wielded the gospel sickle for three weeks, God wonderfully blessed.

"After the Los Angeles campaign," Billy said, "I thought it couldn't happen in Boston. But God did it again in Boston.

Then I thought, 'what God has done in the great cities of Los Angeles and Boston will never happen in the small city of Columbia (population 100,000).' But here in Columbia I have seen the greatest moving of God's Spirit it has ever been my privilege to witness,' he declared. "But I deserve no credit for it! Give all the glory and praise to God."

In three weeks preceding the final Sunday afternoon stadium rally, over 100,000 persons jammed the Columbia Township Auditorium to hear the gospel sung and preached by the Billy Graham party nightly. Of these, 5,050 people went downstairs to the basement prayer room to make decisions for Jesus Christ; approximately 70 per cent were clear-cut professions of faith in Christ as Saviour. The remainder were divided between reconsecration and those entering into assurance of their salvation. In this city of the old south, where the vast majority of the population is nominally affiliated with the church, over 75 per cent of the converts were already church members.

Sunday afternoon, February 19, when the auditorium opened its doors, 3,800 seats were filled long before the starting hour. Hundreds stood, and hundreds more were turned away.

Again that night the auditorium was overflowing at nine p.m. when the meeting began. Contrary to his usual policy, Billy Graham felt the need of the Holy Spirit to give an invitation at the end of his message which was addressed to Christians. God moved down upon the crowd in great conviction, and over 240 made decisions for Christ in that first meeting of the crusade—an event unparalleled in any of the Billy Graham party's experience.

From that night on it was evident that the Spirit of God was putting in the gospel sickle in the city of Columbia. Every single night there were clear-cut decisions for Christ. On no night were there less than a hundred and twenty-five persons coming to Christ. On the third Sunday night when Dr. Graham was resting, Associate Evangelist Grady Wilson brought the message, and 200 again came to Christ.

One earnest Christian who followed up a number of the converts the same week reported that every one she contacted had definite assurance of salvation and was giving evidence of going on with God. Observers believe this alone to be an unusual manifestation of God's blessing on the campaign.

The greatest single reaping of the crusade, apart from its closing Sunday afternoon rally, was the great high school meeting on March 2. Over 4,000 high school and junior high school young people were crowded closely into the auditorium that afternoon. Billy Graham warned them that they were living in the most critical hour in the world's history. He told them of God's hatred for sin, and of the judgment that He would send upon sinners.

When the invitation was given, observers said that they had never seen such a solemn group of young people. There was no undue emotionalism. The aisles were filled with hundreds of teen-agers streaming to the prayer room.

The prayer room was quickly filled and overflowing. The stairs to the prayer room were jammed. Aisles on the edge of the auditorium were crowded. While Grady Wilson spoke to hundreds in the basement auditorium and prayer room, Dr. Graham stood on the steps and spoke to other hundreds in the hall. A newspaper estimated that three to five hundred who responded to the invitation could not get within hearing of the evangelists' voices.

When the meeting was over, 944 had signed decision cards for Jesus Christ. Of these, 739 were first-time, clear-cut decisions to accept Christ as Saviour.

"This is the greatest youth meeting I've been in in my life," Billy said. "I have never seen the Spirit of God deal with a group of young people like this." High school teachers reported that the whole atmosphere in many high schools was different the following morning. High school teachers were seen weeping openly in the halls as the students' attitudes electrified whole schools.

The following week the University of South Carolina students invited the party to speak there. Officials in charge had little faith that the 3500-student university would send more than 500 to hear Billy Graham in the noon hour. The meeting was assigned to the small chapel, seating approximately 400. Long before the hour came, the chapel was jammed to the doors. Hastily-erected seats outside the chapel doors accommodated over five hundred more students. When the invitation was given here, again God gave a great harvest when over 50 raised their hands to profess faith in Christ. Scores more of the University students attended the nightly meetings, and many of these professed Christ as Saviour.

On the final Saturday morning of the crusade, 4,500 boys and girls filled every possible seat in the auditorium to hear "Uncle Cliff" Barrows, "Uncle Grady" Wilson, "Uncle Ted" Smith, "Uncle Bev" Shea, "Uncle Bill" Bernsten, and "Uncle Don" Hoke do magic object lessons, tell Bible stories, sing, and play. Again God moved over these children as Cliff Barrows gave the invitation. Over 500 streamed into the basement prayer room to have explained to them what it meant to accept Christ as Saviour.

Associate Evangelist Grady Wilson held a score of radio broadcasts, preached in the local churches, schools, and civic clubs, and saw hundreds more come to Christ. On the last Sunday morning prior to the stadium rally, 70 persons came to the altar of one of the Baptist churches after his message.

Not only in the auditorium itself, but throughout the entire state the impact of the revival was felt. A radio station in Sumter (South Carolina), 40 miles away, carried the broadcast nightly to an estimated 50,000 people. Citizens reported that "everybody" in Sumter county was listening. Many were saved alongside their radios. The broadcast was the talk of the whole area.

Outstanding coverage by the two Columbia newspapers heightened the spirit of revival across the state. W. Thomas

McMahan, copy editor of *The State* (largest newspaper in South Carolina) and an alumnus of Columbia Bible College, was able from his strategic position to report sympathetically all of the meetings and get the full text of Dr. Graham's sermons in each morning. Reports were received of several conversions from the reading of these newspaper articles.

Revival and salvation were *the* main topics of conversation throughout the city the last two weeks. It was heard on the buses, in the shops, over the telephones, and wherever sinners and saints alike gathered to talk.

Notable among the effects of the crusade was the impact on high government officials. Governor and Mrs. J. Strom Thurmond attended frequently. Early in the second week the Governor declared, "I think the hope of the world today is for more people to turn to Christ. Billy Graham is a great evangelist and is conducting a wonderful meeting in Columbia. We are proud that he is winning so many souls to the Lord."

Justice Jimmy Byrnes, number one citizen of South Carolina in recent years as Secretary of State under the Roosevelt administration, sat next to Dr. Graham on the platform in the Sunday stadium rally. Choked with emotion after the service, he put his arm around Billy Graham and said, "I've been with statesmen, presidents, and kings, but this is the most inspiring moment of my life."

Invited by unanimous resolution to speak before a joint session of the senate and representatives of the state, Dr. Graham warned them that the only hope for salvation for America and the world was a nation-wide spiritual awakening. Following that meeting, many of the legislators attended nightly in a body, and several were converted.

When a knotty problem blocked the senate a few days later, one of the senators arose and said, "Let's do what Billy Graham told us to do; let's pray." The senate was adjourned immediately for a period of prayer.

Henry Luce, publisher of *Life, Time* and *Fortune* magazines flew down to observe the meetings one night of the final week. Much impressed, he told Billy Graham that he believed in what he, Graham, was doing and in what he preached; and he pledged the cooperation of his magazines to support all the subsequent Graham campaigns in other cities. *Life* and *Time* photographers and correspondents covered the great stadium rally.

The first convert of the campaign was led to Christ before the first invitation was ever given. Businessman Cliff Smith, chairman of the Los Angeles campaign of October 1949, flew in to be present on the opening day. After his testimony on Sunday afternoon, his hotel phone rang. At the other end of the line a man's voice said, "If this meant enough to you to fly here from Los Angeles you've got something for me." Meeting him at the auditorium that night before the meeting, Cliff had the opportunity of leading lumber merchant Harry Reynolds to Christ. Then Reynolds began to work on his friend, Colonel Guy V. Whitener, owner of the largest lumber mill in the Carolinas. A week later Whitener came to one meeting. The following night he came again. When the invitation was given that night, Reynolds accompanied Whitener down to the inquiry room where God had providentially placed a returned missionary who led him to full assurance of salvation in Christ.

Sunday afternoon at the closing stadium rally Whitener told reporters, "I want the whole world to know I'm a Christian. I was the biggest sinner in South Carolina for years, now I want people to know that Christ has changed me."

On the second night of the meetings, pitcher Kirby Higbe of the New York Giants, alleged bad boy of the big leagues, came to Christ. A few days later he left for spring training in Phoenix, Arizona. There the Associated Press wire service reported in a few days that he was trying to win his teammates to Christ. He told manager Leo Durocher that there would be no more broken training rules or wild parties for him, he was going all-out for Jesus Christ. Later reports revealed he was witnessing to all of his colleagues and spending two hours a day in Bible study and prayer under the supervision of local Christians.

Loudspeakers mounted outside the auditorium carried the message to hundreds standing outside, or seated in cars, nightly. One night a heavy rain drove an elderly woman into a doorway across the street. As she stood there waiting for the rain to stop, she heard the message. When the invitation was given she got down on her knees in the rain to give her heart to Jesus Christ.

On a porch across the street a Negress had also been driven to shelter from the rain. When the invitation was given she also accepted Christ and came over to the auditorium to make profession of her faith.

Convicted as he read the sermon in the newspaper, a deaf mute came to the final meeting in the auditorium Saturday night, March 11. There one of the personal workers found him, and in an anteroom led him to Christ during the service by writing notes back and forth.

A lawyer drove down from Charlotte for two nights and accepted Christ the first night. A hard-boiled police sergeant of the city police force, a singer in the choir, came to Christ after the first few nights. "It was worth this whole campaign to get me saved," he declared. "God only knows what a sinner I have been."

Throughout the whole state as well as the city, the spirit of revival mounted during the days of the crusade. "I've never seen such hunger on the part of the people for revival," Billy Graham said. "I believe this is just the beginning of a great work of the Holy Spirit that God is going to send throughout the state."

When crowds jammed out the auditorium the first week, plans were proposed to build a 12,000-seat wooden cathedral in the city. When this was deemed inadvisable, Evangelist Billy Graham and his co-workers believed that God was leading them to try to contact the thousands of spiritually-hungry people in the other cities of the state. When his intention was made known, telegrams from mayors, city councils, ministerial associations, and civic clubs flooded from every sizable city throughout the state. Where these invitations were unanimous, as they were in all the larger cities, the team accepted one night engagements for a two-weeks' tour throughout the state beginning Sunday night, March 12.

Again, God moved in these meetings from the very outset. The first Sunday night 4,000 people crowded into the thousand-seat Baptist church at Edgefield, South Carolina. Two hundred and twenty-six came to Christ. The second night, 7,000 people thronged the Augusta (Georgia) city auditorium and hundreds more came to Christ.

In Sumter and Spartanburg, huge outdoor stadiums seating 8,000 and 12,000 people were jammed for afternoon meetings, and God again gave a harvest of souls.

These have been reaping days in South Carolina. As Dr. Billy Graham well said, he did not do this. The Holy Spirit did it. Hundreds of faithful pastors and Christian workers have sowed, watered, and hoed with prayers and tears over the years. And through Dr. Graham, God gave the harvest.

Over and over Billy Graham repeated, "No credit for this belongs to me. There are three reasons why God has given us a great harvest time in Columbia these weeks. The first is, the prayers of those thousands who prayed for one month before we came. The second reason is the power of the Holy Spirit of God in convicting men. And the third is the power of the Word of God. To Him be all the glory."

Not for 27 years has the city of Columbia had a city-wide revival. It nowhere near equalled the impact of this in all the churches. And probably not in the history of South Carolina has there been such a revival harvest of souls as God graciously sent to this city this year.

PREACHING DURING
THE REVIVAL

What did Billy Graham preach during the revival in Los Angeles and Boston? is a question many people have asked. Space forbids reproducing all these sermons, so the publishers have selected six that were greatly used of God to reach men's hearts. They are straight-forward gospel messages, only the gist of which can be reproduced here. It is our prayer that they may continue to be a blessing each time they are read.

The Publishers.

We Need Revival!

"The vision of Isaiah the son of Amoz, which he saw concerning Judah and Jerusalem in the days of Uzziah, Jotham, Ahaz, and Hezekiah, kings of Judah. Hear, O heavens, and give ear, O earth: for the Lord hath spoken, I have nourished and brought up children, and they have rebelled against me. The ox knoweth his owner, and the ass his master's crib; but Israel doth not know, my people doth not consider. Ah sinful nation, a people laden with iniquity, a seed of evil-doers, children that are corrupters: they have forsaken the Lord, they have provoked the Holy One of Israel unto anger, they are gone away backward.

"Why should ye be stricken any more? ye will revolt more and more: the whole head is sick, and the whole heart faint. From the sole of the foot even unto the head there is no soundness in it; but wounds, and bruises, and putrifying sores: they have not been closed, neither bound up, neither mollified with ointment. Your country is desolate, your cities are burned with fire: your land, strangers devour it in your presence, and it is desolate, as overthrown by strangers. And the daughter of Zion is left as a cottage in a vineyard, as a lodge in a garden of cucumbers, as a besieged city. Except the Lord of hosts had left unto us a very small remnant, we should have been as Sodom, and we should have been like unto Gomorrah.

"Hear the word of the Lord, ye rulers of Sodom; give ear unto the law of our God, ye people of Gomorrah. To what purpose is the multitude of your sacrifices unto me? saith the Lord: I am full of the burnt offerings of rams, and the fat of fed beasts; and I delight not in the blood of bullocks, or of lambs, or of he goats. When ye come to appear before me, who hath required this at your hand, to tread my courts? Bring no more vain oblations; incense is an abomination unto me; the new moons and sabbaths, the calling of assemblies, I cannot away with; it is iniquity, even the solemn meeting. Your new moons and your appointed feasts my soul hateth: they are a trouble unto me; I am weary to bear them. And when ye spread forth your hands, I will hide mine eyes from you: yea, when ye make many prayers, I will not hear: your hands are full of blood.

"Wash you, make you clean; put away the evil of your doings from before mine eyes; cease to do evil. Learn to do well; seek judgment, relieve the oppressed, judge the fatherless, plead for the widow. Come now, and let us reason together, saith the Lord: though your sins be as scarlet, they shall be as white as snow; though they be red like crimson, they shall be as wool. If ye be willing and obedient, ye shall eat the good of the land: But if ye refuse and rebel, ye shall be devoured with the sword: for the mouth of the Lord hath spoken it" (Isa. 1:1-20).

I WANT to speak on the subject, "The Choice that is Before Los Angeles During these Next Three Weeks." Remember the verse we just read, "Except the Lord of hosts had left unto us a very small remnant, we should have been as Sodom, and we should have been like unto Gomorrah."

I have been in Europe six times since the war and have seen devastated cities of Germany and the wreckage of war. I believe the only reason that America escaped the ravages and destruction of war was because God's people prayed. Many of these people believe that God can still use America to evangelize the world. I think that we are living at a time in world history when God is giving us a desperate choice, a choice of either revival or judgment. There is no other alternative! And I particularly believe this applies to the city of Los Angeles—this city of wickedness and sin, this city that is known around the world because of its sin, crime and immorality. God Almighty is going to bring judgment upon this city unless people repent and believe—unless God sends an old-fashioned, heaven-sent, Holy Ghost revival.

How desperately we need revival! Think, for a moment, of some of the dreadful things happening throughout the western world. On Friday morning the entire world was shocked. (Sept. 23, 1949.) Across Europe at this very hour there is stark, naked fear among the people, for we all realize that war is much closer than we ever dreamed. The people of Europe stand on the threshold of the unknown. Our President, at the same time as did Prime Minister Clement Attlee in London, announced to the startled world that Russia has now exploded an atomic bomb. An arms race, unprecedented in the history of the world, is driving us madly toward destruction! And I sincerely believe that it is the providence of God that He has chosen this hour for a campaign—giving this city one more chance to repent of sin and turn to a believing knowledge of the Lord Jesus Christ.

Recalling again our subject, Los Angeles' choice, see the need for a decision in the philosophical realm. The era of Materialism, Paganism and Humanism has been emphasized in the educational circles of this country. Man has steered our course. We have been humanizing God. Throughout our land we have denied the supernatural, outlawed the supernatural, and said that miracles are not now possible. We are taken up with *things* rather than with the *Spirit of God*.

Then look at our moral standard. There was a time a few years ago, which most of you with gray hair can remember, when this country claimed the Ten Commandments as the basis for our moral code. That is no longer true. Last year we had one divorce to every three-and-a-half marriages. Thirty years ago we had one divorce to every twenty-five marriages. The home, the basic unit of our society is breaking and crumbling, and the American way of life is being destroyed at the very heart and core of society.

At the same time we see an unchecked crime wave in this country. Your mayor recently told the editors of *Quick* magazine that crime in Los Angeles is out of hand. For the first time in many years a great metropolitan city has asked the Federal government to take over because there is so much crime. We need revival! Eight hundred per cent increase in crime in the last ten years in Los Angeles.

Look at the problem of sex. Everywhere, but especially emphasized and underscored here, we see sex placed before American young people. If we want to sell even a motor car tire, we have to use sex to do it. As a result, our high school and college young people are going to the dogs morally—encouraged by the press and radio across this Nation. We need a revival!

At the same time, gambling is going on from one end of this city to the other. Behind locked doors, there is wide-open, flagrant disobedience to the laws of this city. Our young people are gambling and being instructed in it every hour of the day. We need revival!

The mayor has said that one of the problems in this town is too many cocktail bars—there are more cocktail bars than there are policemen in the city of Los Angeles. He said, "We don't have enough policemen to check on the liquor situation and, as a result, our city is drinking its way to destruction." Think of that! Three million chronic alcoholics in America today—thousands of them in the city of Los Angeles. We need a revival!

Let's turn to the teen-age delinquency problem. Do you know the age group having the greatest number of arrests last year? The greatest number of arrests last year in the city of Los Angeles was of seventeen-year-old boys and girls.

Let us look for a moment at the political realm. Let's see what is happening—not only in the city of Los Angeles, but in the western world. The world is divided into two sides. On the one side we see Communism; on the other side we see so-called Western culture. Western culture and its fruit had its foundation in the Bible, the Word of God, and in the revivals of the Seventeenth and Eighteenth Centuries. Communism, on the other hand, has decided against God, against Christ, against the Bible, and against all religion. Communism is not only an economic interpretation of life—Communism is a religion that is inspired, directed and motivated by the Devil himself who has declared war against Almighty God. Do you know that the Fifth Columnists, called Communists, are more rampant in Los Angeles than any other city in America? We need a revival.

Now for the first time in the history of the world we have the weapon with which to destroy ourselves—the atomic bomb. I am persuaded that time is desperately short! Three months ago, in the House of Parliament, a British statesman told me that the British government feels we have only five to ten years and our civilization will be ended. That was before he heard that Russia has the atomic bomb.

Recently I saw an educational film entitled "No Place to Hide." It is a picture story of what would happen if the germ bombs and poison bombs and atomic bombs were loosed on civilization. There would not be much left after such a bombing! We need a Holy Ghost, heaven-sent revival!

Let us look at the religious world for a moment. In this city Satan has succeeded in working his favorite strategy—counterfeiting the true gospel of our Lord Jesus Christ. We find more false prophets and cults than in any other place in all the world. The god of this age is blinding people. Demon power is felt as you walk down the streets of this city. A Gallup poll shows that 95% of the people of Los Angeles say they believe in God, but do you know how many are identified with any church? Twenty-seven per cent of the people of Los Angeles County identify themselves with a church. Do you know how many go to church more than once a year? Only eight per cent. Ninety-five per cent believe in God! Only eight per cent go to church more than once a year! There is desperate need of evangelism and prayer that God will send a revival so that people may become conscious of the tremendous issues that face us today. We need revival!

I wish we had time to go on with other statistics, but I do want to say that underlying every word I have to say is the basic law of God—"The wages of sin is death." If Sodom and Gomorrah could not get away with sin; if Pompeii and Rome could not escape, neither can Los Angeles! Judgment is coming as sure as I am standing here! Unless God's people turn to Him and the city repents, we are going to see the judgment of God come upon us.

A great many pastors tell me that, while they can't explain it or understand exactly why, they sincerely believe that this great united effort is God's plan for the city of Los Angeles. They feel that if we do not repent of sin and turn to Him while there is time, there will be no other great opportunity like this. Our responsibility as Christians during these days is tremendous! I have prayed more, and have spent more time with God than I ever have in any other city; and I am asking God's people to pray; to be faithful in attending these services and to bring others that many may come to believe in the Lord Jesus Christ.

This may be God's last great call! Look at the cities of the past that had their opportunities. The antediluvian civilization heard Noah as he stood and preached repentance. For 120 years people scoffed and did not repent. You know what God said? "My Spirit shall not always strive with man." And He said, "It repented me that I ever made man." Then judgment came upon the great civilization of Noah's day.

The peoples of Sodom and Gomorrah heard Abraham and Lot ask them to repent. But they refused and fire and brimstone from the hand of God rained down upon those cities.

Nazareth had the opportunity of hearing the most blessed and most wonderful Spirit-filled Preacher of all time—the Lord Jesus Christ. But because of the unbelief and sin of the people, He did no great works in Nazareth. Many people of that day died and went to hell.

One day the Apostle Paul passed by the city of Pompeii. The sin and immorality of Pompeii was known throughout the

Roman Empire. Pompeii would not listen nor repent; and God caused Vesuvius to erupt. The city was destroyed and every living thing in the city.

God spared not those great cities. Neither will God spare this city! I warn you to repent of sin and turn to Jesus Christ as a city before it is too late. Do you know what God is going to do? One of these days—it may not be this year, it may be a hundred years from now, I do not know the time, but I do know this—unless we have a revival, one of these little tremors that you call an earthquake may shake every building in Los Angeles. Under the judging hand of God, a tidal wave may sweep across this city, unless we repent of our sin. Do you know the area that is marked out for the enemy's first atomic bomb? New York! Secondly, Chicago; and thirdly, the city of Los Angeles! We don't know how soon, but we do know this, that right now the grace of God can still save a poor lost sinner. We know that the gates of heaven are still open to those who will repent and believe that Jesus is God's Son and our Saviour.

Somebody asked me the other day whether I think we can have a revival. What a foolish question! Some people say that apostasy is too deep, the picture is too black, and it is impossible to have a revival. They say that sin is too rampant, that a revival in 1949 is impossible.

I tell you, beloved, it was a dark day and a mighty dreary picture when Jonah went to Nineveh. The sins that I have mentioned this afternoon existed in the city of Nineveh; but Nineveh repented and the judgment of God that was about to fall, was held back. Nineveh was spared the judgment of Almighty God.

In this moment I can see the judgment hand of God over Los Angeles. I can see judgment about to fall. If we repent, if we believe, if we turn to Christ in faith and hope, the judgment of God can be stopped. From the depths of my heart, I believe that this message is God's word today.

It was a dark hour when Elijah climbed to the top of Mount Carmel—all the prophets of Baal were against him, the king and queen opposed him, the army was his enemy: he was alone! There were 7,000 people that did believe, but they were hiding in caves, afraid. Only one man dared to believe God would send a revival. Seven thousand people said, "It can't be done." "Everything and everyone is against you!" they told Elijah.

People, often God's children, say the same thing today. Let me tell you that nothing is too hard for our God!

But they had a revival in Elijah's day! On top of Mount Carmel the prophets of Baal called on their god. There was no response—he was off on a fishing trip and couldn't hear them, or he had gone off somewhere else and couldn't hear. Elijah called upon God to rain down fire. The fire fell, and revival came to the men of Israel. In a few days, Ahab and Jezebel were taken from the throne and God was given His rightful place in the land of Israel.

Look at the day when Hezekiah came to the throne. Old Ahaz his father was walking around like he owned the world. His shoulders were thrown back; he was proud and cocky, a fellow who believed in idols and who worshipped the god of the trees and the god of the sun; a fellow that had set up other gods and had denied the Lord God of Israel. Then Hezekiah came to the throne; called upon the people to repent and to turn to God. Revival took place in a dark and black hour in the history of Judah.

It was a dark hour when John Wesley and George Whitefield preached the gospel, but England had a revival! That country was saved from the fate of the French Revolution.

God said, "If my people, which are called by my name, shall humble themselves, and pray, and seek my face, and turn from their wicked ways; then will I hear from heaven, and will forgive their sin, and will heal their land" (II Chron. 7:14). Do you believe that? I believe that we can have revival any time we meet God's conditions. I believe that God is true to His Word, and that He must rain righteousness upon us if we meet His conditions.

What are His conditions? First, realization of need and a desire for revival. I am talking to Christians now. Do you want a revival today? Would you like to see this city moved from center to circumference? Would you like God to bless us and people turn to Him? Would you like Hollywood to be so shaken that it might influence the world for Christ? Would you like the Spirit of God in our midst as He has never been before? We can have it! I say we can have it, if we meet God's conditions!

The second condition for revival is repentance. Scripture says, "If I regard iniquity in my heart, the Lord will not hear me" (Ps. 66:18). Do you know what repentance is? Repentance is confession of sin, repentance is sorrow for sin, and repentance is renouncing sin. Many people say they believe God's Word and accept Christ's sacrifice, but they have never been truly repentant! If they were, their lives would show it.

And then the third thing is to pray. Revival never comes except in answer to prayer. A few months ago the city of Augusta, Georgia, was moved upon by the Spirit of God. Do you know why? Before we ever arrived, there were 13,000 prayer meetings held in that city. God was moving before we got there, in answer to prayer.

Do you know what prayer implies? Prayer implies that we must be in one accord. That means we can't have divisions among us. That means that if I am a Presbyterian or you are a Baptist, or if I am a Baptist or a Pentecostal, regardless of denomination, we have to forget our differences—forget any minor points of argument and join together around the cross of the Lord Jesus Christ. We must unite in prayer and supplication to the Lord, and God will send a revival. That means that we have to love one another, and our hearts must be bound together. When we love one another, there won't be any pride. When we love one another, there won't be any jealousy. When we love one another, there won't be any envy. When we love one another, there won't be any gossip. When we really love one another, there won't be any of these sins, because love binds us together and presents us to God in the purity of Christ.

Fourth, in order to have a revival we must have faith. Unbelief is a sin that keeps back revival in city after city because people will not believe God's Word and take Him at His word. God says if we meet certain conditions, He *will* send a revival; He *will* send the blessing, and sinners will turn to Him. We have to take God at His word and not doubt Him. We need revival!

Now, what are the results of revival? The church will be on fire, burning with a desire to serve Him. Christians will be compelled to bring others to know Him.

There will be a new missionary emphasis in the church. We will turn our eyes on a world that is lost and dying and going to hell because these souls have not accepted God's plan. Prayer meetings will be jammed, people will love the hour of prayer and spend time in communion with God. The church will add new members. I believe that any work, any campaign, any evangelistic effort that is not contributing to the church is not building a lasting foundation in that place. God has approved the organization of the churches, and we are praying that thousands of people will be swept into the church during the days while we are here.

Wouldn't it be great to see the members of the church filled with the Holy Ghost? They will be if revival comes. "Ye shall receive power, after that the Holy Ghost is come upon you" (Acts 1:8). Not only will the church members be revived, but many more will accept the Lord Jesus Christ.

Fourteen years ago, down in the city of Charlotte, North Carolina, the ministers of our town forgot their differences; the laymen, together with the ministers, held a city-wide evangelistic campaign. Do you know one of the things that attracted me? I saw the people who, a few days before, had been quick to argue with one another, now joined together around the cross of Jesus Christ. I said, "If that is taking place, there must be something to Christianity." I went to the services and was converted in an old-fashioned revival meeting just like this. When we join hands and the gospel is preached under the anointing and power of the Holy Ghost, revival comes and souls will turn to believe on the Lord Jesus Christ.

Finally, a revival brings tremendous social implications. Do you know what came out of past revivals? The abolishment of slavery came out of revival. The abolishment of child labor came out of revival. When the Wesleys preached in England, people were working ninety hours a week! As a result of that revival, sixty working hours became standard, and our great trade unions were organized. Did you know that the Y.M.C.A., the Salvation Army, most of our charity organizations, many of our educational institutions, slum clearance programs, the Sunday School, Christian reform and Women's Suffrage are revival results?

Now, in closing, to you Christians, you that profess the name of the Lord Jesus Christ—if this is going to be just another campaign, if we are going to take it half-heartedly, we might as well stop right now. But this may be God's last call to Los Angeles! I am going to ask you to make your business secondary, to make your family secondary, to make everything else secondary for three weeks. Try God, believe God, prove God and come to these meetings. Pray and work as if your life and soul depended on it. Then watch God work during these days, that this opportunity given to Los Angeles—the choice of accepting or rejecting Christ—may not be in vain.

This same choice must be made by every person here this afternoon without Christ. Your choice can be one of two decisions—accept Christ and believe Him, or die without Him and suffer judgment at the Great White Throne Judgment. At that time God says those whose names are not written in the Lamb's Book of Life will be cast into the lake of fire.

What can you do? Right now you can turn to Jesus. Let Christ come into your heart and cleanse you from sin, and He can give you the assurance that if you died tonight, you would go to heaven. We call this belief in Christ salvation—*anyone* can be saved by simply believing that the Lord Jesus Christ suffered and died for his sin. Right now you can know that you are going to heaven. Will you accept Him?

Calling all Los Angeles to the Evangelistic services in the "Canvas Cathedral" under Billy Graham was this large sign facing the nearby thoroughfare. The Sunday evening service was set at 8:45 to give people an opportunity to attend early services at their own churches.

Pictorial Sidelights
of the Los Angeles Revival

When the "Canvas Cathedral" was packed to capacity, thousands of interested and eager people stood on the sidewalk outside to hear the message over loudspeakers.

GREATER
LOS ANGELES
'B... GRAHAM

Something's Happening Inside
Continuing **ANOTHER WEEK**

6000
free SEATS

HUNDREDS
of CHURCHES

NIGHTLY 7:30
SUNDAYS 3–8:45

This is the way (above) the continuation of the Los Angeles campaign was announced to the passing public and below is a view inside the huge tent which seated 6,000 people. A veritable "Canvas Cathedral."

Evangelist Billy Graham (far right) and song leader Cliff Barrows (far left) have a word with four converts of the Los Angeles campaign. From left to right after Cliff Barrows: Harvey Fritts, television star heard every Sunday from 2:15 to 2:45 P.M., on KFI-TV; Jim Vaus, underworld wire-tapper who had worked with the most notorious underworld characters; Stuart Hamblen, director of radio program "Stuart Hamblen and His Lucky Stars," heard on Warner Brothers Radio Station KFWB Hollywood, who in 1936 won the western championship rodeo title before 35,000 at Gilmore Stadium, in Los Angeles, who is also composer of hundreds of folk songs; Louis Zamperini, member of the 1936 American Olympic Team which competed in Berlin, Germany, and holder of collegiate record in the mile, war hero who spent 47 days on a life raft and 14 months in Japanese prison camps.

Billy Graham confers with (left) Mayor Fletcher Bowron of Los Angeles.

Two of the leaders of the Los Angeles revival: Clifford Smith (right), president of the Christ for Greater Los Angeles Campaign, and executive secretary Claude Jenkins.

I. A. "Daddy" Moon, director of personal work at the Los Angeles campaign and who had a prayer tent accommodating 500 people, here writes down on his decision cards the names and addresses of two children who made decisions during the evangelistic meetings.

On the final night of the Boston campaign the crowd overflowed Boston Gardens with 16,000 people, leaving several thousand standing outside to listen to the message and the meeting over the loudspeakers. The gates were closed at 7:00 o'clock.

Boston's Revival Overflows
City's Largest Hall

The overflow crowd on the outside of Mechanics Hall in Boston which could not get in and to which Billy Graham spoke preceeding his message inside.

Without fanfare or emotionalism, Billy Graham gave a very simple invitation to those who wanted to accept Christ to come forward, and this is the result. So many crowded to the front that they were directed to a room at the side which would accommodate 2,000 people. Before long it was filled. This view was taken during the invitation.

Inside Mechanics Hall the Boston meetings continued for the largest part of three weeks, indicating just how intense was the interest and how heavy the attendance.

Billy Graham and Mrs. Graham are pictured with Dr. Harold Ockenga, pastor of Park Street Church and who for a decade had been praying earnestly that revival might come to conservative, intellectual, unregenerate Boston.

The Opera House was the next meeting place after Park Street Church, but this building could not hold the crowd and it went to Mechanics Hall.

Leaders in the work of the Boston revival campaign from left to right: John Lincoln, in charge of personal work; Allan Emery, Jr., general chairman of the committee; Gordon Sanders, in charge of publicity. These men worked tirelessly, practically day and night, both before and during the campaign.

Billy Graham here extends his appreciation for cooperation and prayer interest in the campaign to three college and Bible institute presidents. From right to left: Howard Ferrin, president, Providence Bible Institute, Providence, Rhode Island; Dr. T. Leonard Lewis, president, Gordon School of Theology; Dr. Paul Vanech, New England School of Theology.

The Home God Honors

"And whatsoever ye do in word or deed, do all in the name of the Lord Jesus, giving thanks to God and the Father by him. Wives, submit yourselves unto your own husbands, as it is fit in the Lord. Husbands, love your wives, and be not bitter against them. Children, obey your parents in all things: for this is well pleasing unto the Lord. Fathers, provoke not your children to anger, lest they be discouraged" (Col. 3:17-21).

MANY YEARS ago Henry Grady, that great southern statesman, stood before the Capitol at Washington, D.C. and said to himself, "This is the heart of America." Then as he stood there he said, "It seemed that the great Nation's building faded and in its place I saw a little home down in the mountains of North Carolina. As I thought of that little home down there, I saw a poor, rugged, sun-tanned father with calloused hands. Every evening he called his children to gather around the old family Bible and have their family worship and family prayers." Then Grady said, "I remembered how father would awaken us at sunrise every morning, call us out of bed to say family prayers. At every meal we had family grace. Father plowed in the fields all the day long. His hands were calloused; his face was sun-tanned; perspiration streamed down his brow, but he was an honest man and he reared his children in the fear and nurture and admonition of the Lord. As I stood there and saw that scene, I realized that the foundation of American society and the very heart and core of America is the American home."

Tonight I'm convinced that the basic unit of our society is the home. I'm also convinced that when the home begins to lose its hold on our lives and to disintegrate, then our society is on the way out.

The word "home" recalls a thousand memories in our minds and in our hearts. As long as I live I'll never forget my own home. I'll never forget my father and mother. They reared their children in the fear of the Lord. I never heard my parents argue. I do not even remember their using a slang word, much less a word of profanity. My father and mother prayed for their children and tonight all of their children know the Lord Jesus Christ as personal Saviour. They brought us up around the old family Bible.

The first institution ever established was the home. Before the church, before the school, before the government, God established the home. The first marriage ceremony was performed by God Himself in the Garden of Eden. Today in America we have thirty-one million homes. Tonight almost every person in Los Angeles will go to some place that he calls home — the scores that are on the street, in places of amusement — even those down on Skid Row. The very basis of our entire way of life is built upon the home. Rich or poor, whatever color or nationality, we call some place home. It may be a cottage or a palace, but we call it home. A home reaches right into the very center of our being. The word stirs a thousand memories of days of yesteryear, when we remember father, mother, the family circle.

"Mid pleasures and palaces, though we may roam,
  Be it ever so humble, there's no place like home;
  A charm from the sky seems to hallow us there,
  Which, seek through the world, is ne'er met with elsewhere. . . .

"An exile from home, splendor dazzles in vain,
  O, give me my lowly thatched cottage again!
  The birds singing gayly, that came at my call—
  Give me them,—and the piece of mind, dearer than all! . . .

"How sweet 'tis to sit 'neath a fond father's smile,
  And the cares of a mother to soothe and beguile!
  Let others delight 'mid new pleasure to roam,
  But give me, O, give me, the pleasures of home. . . .

"To thee I'll return, overburdened with care;
  The heart's dearest solace will smile on me there;
  No more from that cottage again will I roam;
  Be it ever so humble, there's no place like home.
  Home, Home, sweet, sweet Home! There's no place like home!
  There's no place like Home."

Jesus had a lowly birth. Jesus not only loved His home but He loved the home of Mary and Lazarus. Jesus went to many homes and sanctified the home by His own presence and by His own endorsement. But tonight as we look at America's needs and the social problems of our great Nation, we find that the greatest problem confronting the present world today is not Communism. The greatest problem confronting us tonight is the breakdown of the American home. Sometimes I wonder who is going to win the race to capture America — whether it is going to be Communism or whether it is going to be mold and deterioration that's starting in the American home and is eating out the heart and soul of our society.

A nation is only as strong as her homes. The greatest men of our day were not fashioned on battlefields but in the cradle and the fireside of their childhood homes. Our country should fear disloyalty and contention at the fireside more than any political force because the very root and the very foundation, the heart and the soul of our society, is the home. Satan's chief aim today is to destroy the home. One of the goals of Communism is to destroy the American home. If the Communist can destroy the American home and cause moral deterioration in this country, that group will have done to us what they did to France when the German armies invaded the Maginot line. From what I have seen in Europe since the war I am convinced that the thing which caused the defeat of France in 1940 was not the German army. It was the moral deterioration of France before the Germans ever came. The same thing is happening in America tonight. I'm not afraid of what Joe Stalin can do with his atomic bomb, I'm not afraid of what he can do with his copy of the B-36. I'm not so afraid tonight of what poison bombs will do as I am afraid of what Satan is doing to destroy the morals of America and to break down our homes. When our homes break, our Nation is crumbling to the same ruin as other empires, other cities and other nations, because they, too, were peoples with broken homes.

In America, one million people receive divorces *every year*: five hundred thousand divorces a year. One divorce to every 3½ marriages in America last year. France had only one-fourth the number of divorces that we have, Germany had only one-third the divorces we have, Japan had only one-half the divorces that we have. I say tonight, our major problem is the home. If we can solve our marital problems and save our homes, we have solved the major problem in the American way of life.

Tonight, there are many major enemies of the home. Satan, of course, is an enemy of the home. And if Satan can cause contention and strife and sin and unfaithfulness in the home, he's going to win the first bout in his battle to gain the home. Selfishness is an enemy of the home; unfaithfulness is an enemy of the home; alcohol is an enemy of the home; maladjustment is an enemy of the home; and jealousy is an enemy of the home. Much of our church, radio and spirit of the day has made a laughing stock of marriage until Americans have lost the sanctity of marriage, and have lost sight of the fact that God instituted marriage.

I am convinced, that there is only one thing halting the destruction of the American way of life, and that is the existence of Christian institutions. How long can they hold the water back? Here we have waters of sin, juvenile delinquency, divorce and broken homes piling up and the dam of Christian institutions is trying to hold the waters back, but already I can see cracks. I can see crevices and I can see the water dripping through. One of these days the dam is going to break and the waters are going to flood America. We will have no more America, unless God can visit us with an old-fashioned, heaven-sent, Holy

Ghost revival. That's the answer to our problems tonight. There seems to be no other answer except revival.

But tonight I want to turn to God's word. We have turned to the psychiatrist, and we've turned to the psychologist and we have all sorts of books on the home. We have all kinds of books on how to rear children. We have all kinds of psychological books and documents and surveys and now, to top it all, we have the *Kinsey Report*. We have many different attempts aimed at educating Americans to have happy homes, but there are more unhappy homes today than ever before in our history. Psychology and the psychiatrist do not have the answers. Neither does Mr. Anthony.

Tonight I want you to turn to God's Word and first see the responsibility of each member of the home. First of all I want you to see the responsibility of the wife. Listen to this— "Wives, submit yourselves unto your own husbands, as it is fit in the Lord." Wives, submit yourselves to your husbands. Now that's going to shock some of you wives—some of you who "wear the trousers" in your family, some of you dictatorial wives. But this is the Word of God. Listen to it tonight and see if obedience to God's Word is the way to a happy home life.

One of the problems of the home today is that it is not properly governed. God has certain governing laws for marriage and the home. One of the problems in Christian circles, and the reason we have so many unhappy Christian homes, is because we have forgotten God's laws about marriage. We need them re-emphasized; we need to underscore them; we need to read them. Every family ought to get these passages of Scripture and read them on their knees. Don't stop there—then follow them! Don't be hearers only, but doers of the Word.

The first thing that God says is for wives to submit themselves to their own husbands. That doesn't mean that the husband is to be a tyrant. It conveys the idea of unselfish service and unending loyalty, and that is exactly what it means. Christ is the head of the church, and the husband is the head of the wife. Now the relationship between wife and husband is both and at the same time equal and unequal. It is equal as far as her intellect, her conscience, her position, her service, her freedom, her happiness is concerned before God, because God says, "They twain shall be one flesh."

It's not a question of who is superior, both are superior in God's given place. If a woman conforms to God's standard for a woman, she is superior in her place; if a man conforms to God's standard for a man, he is superior in his place. Now Scripture says this, "Unto the woman he said, I will greatly multiply thy sorrow and thy conception; in sorrow thou shalt bring forth children; and thy desire shall be to thy husband, and he shall rule over thee" (Gen. 3:16). Because of sin in the Garden of Eden, one of the curses God sent upon the woman was that the man shall rule over her. That curse has never been removed nor changed; it has been underlined and underscored all the way through the New Testament.

"Wives, submit yourselves unto your own husbands, as unto the Lord. For the husband is the head of the wife, even as Christ is the head of the church: and he is the saviour of the body. Therefore, as the church is subject unto Christ, so let the wives be to their own husbands in every thing" (Eph. 5:22-24). It does not say "part of the time"—it says "in every thing." In Ephesians 5:33 we read these words: ". . . and the wife see that she reverence her husband." That is a command from the Lord God that the wife reverence her husband. Then in I Peter 3:1, 2 we read these words: "Likewise, ye wives, be in subjection to your own husbands; that, if any obey not the the word, they also may without the word be won by the conversation of the wives; While they behold your chaste conversation coupled with fear." Peter says this when he speaks of a wife who is a Christian and a husband who is not a Christian.

Some time ago a woman said to me, "My husband is not a Christian. Should I obey him and be subject to him?" The

Bible says a decided, "Yes." Here is God's law; here is God's rule—"Don't preach to your husband all the time. Don't nag him to death by preaching to him." It says, "Live in front of him that they also with the Word may be won by the life of the wife." In other words, you are to live a consistent, holy, Christian life in front of your husband and he, seeing the difference, will be convicted of his sin and in time come to Jesus Christ. I've seen so many wives run their husbands away from God in their eagerness to see the one they love come to Christ. They nag and preach so long that the husband is driven away. God's principle is to live an example before unbelieving husbands, rather than preach to them all the time.

Now, Scripture says in Titus 2:4, 5, "That they may teach the young women to be sober, to love their husbands, to love their children. To be discreet, chaste, keepers at home, good, obedient to their own husbands, that the word of God be not blasphemed." Now, notice the language here. Notice these words—be obedient to, reverence and then love and the Bible says if you're not doing these things, if the woman is disobedient on this point, God's Word will be blasphemed in the whole community.

The Scriptures say to love your husband. When he comes home in the evening, run out and meet him and give him a kiss. Give him love at any cost. Cultivate modesty and the delicacy of youth. Be attractive. Read as much as you can to keep up on world events and developments.

Keep the house clean and make sure that you're a good housekeeper. Don't be a spendthrift. You know, if some women died the only thing their husbands would miss would be the first-of-the-month bills. Don't keep your husband's nose to the grindstone all the time, and don't spend all of his money.

Don't nag and complain all the time. Did you ever see a nagging wife? Nag, nag, nag, and complain, complain, complain, all the time? I'll tell you I feel sorry for some of these husbands. Then some wives are on the go all the time. They are never home. God said, "Abraham, where's Sarah?" "Oh, Sarah is out to the theatre." Did he say that? No.

"She's over to the card party." No. "She's over to the ladies auxiliary." No. "Sarah is right here at home where she ought to be."

God meant for women to be home and to rear the children rather than to be running all over the country.

Then another suggestion I have tonight, for both husband and wife—don't gossip. You know that some children have roast preacher every Sunday for dinner? If you parents want to talk about your neighbors, do it in private. Don't do it at all, but if you must, wait until the children are in bed. Gossip is a sin in the sight of God.

Make your house a pleasant place to be. Keep your children interested in the home. Let them invite their friends and keep your home, rather the corner tavern, a center of interest and activity.

Now all you husbands have been sitting there enjoying every bit of this. But I want you to listen to this. Because in Ephesians 5:23 it says this: "For the husband is the head of the wife, even as Christ is the head of the church: and he is the saviour of the body." Joshua said, "As for me and my house, we will serve the Lord." Now listen, where's man's place in the home? Man is God's representative. It is a great responsibility to be the head of a home, for you are responsible to God. You are the protector; you are the provider of the home. Too many men have neglected the home for the club, the lodge, the theatre or the tavern. They have too much pleasure in making money to rear their children in the fear of the Lord.

The Scriptures say to honor your wife. "Likewise, ye husbands, dwell with them according to knowledge, giving honor unto the wife, as unto the weaker vessel, and as being heirs together of the grace of life; that your prayers be not hindered" (I Pet. 3:7). If you fail to honor your wife, your prayers will go unanswered. God can't hear you if you are falling down in your job as a husband. This is God's command—the husband and wife shall dwell together as heirs of the grace of life.

Show your wife that you love her. Don't let love be taken for granted—send her a box of candy once in awhile. Send her an orchid. How long has it been since you sent some roses to your sweetheart?

God's Word says: "Nevertheless let every one of you in particular love his wife as himself" (Eph. 5:33). How do you compare with God's standard? Do you love your wife even as yourself? Believe me, if every husband did, some things would surely be different!

If you love your wife, she won't have to do all the work. I went to a home some time ago and a man who weighed 300 pounds sat down in a great big chair and said, "Lois does the work around here as a woman should." His wife came in. She was a little, over-worked woman, about ready for the grave. He'd just about killed her. Then some of you men, help bear your wife's burdens. She has a hard job. Listen, I'd rather plow in the field all day long than to stay at home and cook three meals and take care of the children one hour. I'll tell you I would. That's a hard job. The woman has a harder job.

Some of you husbands are inclined to be tightwads. Don't pinch the pennies and keep them in the bank waiting for you to die and leave for your children or for somebody to fight over. Let your wife buy a new hat and dress once in awhile.

Be a gentleman; be courteous; be thoughtful. Do the little things that you know women like. It's not the big thing, but it's in consistent small ways that you show love and appreciation.

When a woman marries, she loses much of her own life in that of her husband. Marriage is only part of his life. But to a woman it's everything. Your wife gave up everything to come with you. Remember that, and remember the marriage vows that you took at the altar. You know, it would be good for all of us to take out the old marriage vows and read them over and over again about three or four times a week. It'd make a big difference to both husband and wife, wouldn't it? "Husbands, love your wives, even as Christ also loved the church, and gave himself for it. So ought men to love their wives as their own bodies. He that loveth his wife, loveth himself, nevertheless, let every one of you in particular so love his wife even as himself and the wife see that she reverence her husband."

It's the husband's job to be the head of the home in religious matters. If you don't have a family altar in your home, it's the husband's fault. It is not the wife's responsibility, it's the husband's responsibility unto God to be the head of his home and to call his little family together and rear them around the Word of God. The desperate need of the hour in Christian circles is the old-fashioned family altar. If you don't have a family altar in your home; if you don't have prayer in your home; if you don't have grace at the table, you ought to be ashamed of yourself for your sin against God. Start your family altar. If you've never done it, start a family altar when you get home tonight. It will make all the difference in the world. Every problem that you face in your family will be solved if you can pray together. That's the husband's responsibility unto God. I don't think God will ever hold a woman responsible, it's the husband before God, as God's representative, as the head of the home, who should establish the family altar. Listen, this business of being a father and a husband is a serious business in the sight of God. We've made a big joke out of it. We laugh about it, but in the sight of God it has tremendous repercussions and implications.

You remember the story of Eli. Eli was one of God's servants and Eli refused to restrain his children and make them obey him. He refused to take his proper place in the home. Listen to what God did to him. "In that day, I will perform against Eli all the things which I have spoken concerning his house: when I begin, I will also make an end. For I have told him that I will judge his house forever for the iniquity which he knoweth; because his sons made themselves vile, and he restrained them not" (I Sam. 3:12, 13).

God says, "The father is to be the head of the discipline, the head of correction, the head of the family altar. If the father doesn't take his responsibility, God Almighty is going to judge him and hold him responsible. Eli refused to take his responsibility and God said, "I'm going to judge his house forever because he didn't take his place at the head of the home."

Now all you boys and girls that have been sitting there taking it all in, we're coming to you soon. Because Scripture says, "Children, obey your parents in all things." How many things? All things. "For this is well pleasing unto the Lord." You know what the Devil's philosophy is today? Do as you please. Kick up your heels. Modern psychology is going along with the present program and psychologists are saying, "Don't spank your children, you'll warp their personality." I stand here before you tonight in a warped personality because I got plenty of spanking. I might not have received much head learning down in the hills of North Carolina, but there's one thing I got. There are plenty of callouses on my backbone that were put there by a razor strap. If you haven't had that kind of discipline in your home, you'd better start it, because God demands it. Our children tonight are roaming the streets because there is no home discipline or restraint. Our courts and our jails are filled; juvenile homes are crowded; our Nation is almost "going to the dogs" because our young people have been undisciplined. We need to come back to the Bible to see what It has to say.

In Ephesians 6:4 (R.V.) is this: "And, ye fathers, provoke not your children to wrath: but nurture them in the chastening and admonition of the Lord." In Hebrews 12:7 "If ye endure chastening, God dealeth with you as with sons; for what son is he whom the father chasteneth not?" In Proverbs 13:24 "He that spareth his rod hateth his son:" In other words, God says,

"If you don't correct your child and if you don't give him the spankings he needs once in awhile, you hate your child—you don't love him." Billy Graham didn't say that—God says that in His Word.

"But he that loveth him, chasteneth him often times" (Prov. 19:18). "Chasten thy son while there is hope, and let not thy soul spare for his crying." In other words he may cry; he may weep; he may be broken-hearted, but God says, "Discipline and chasten, and whip if necessary to get the child to learn obedience."

"The rod and reproof give wisdom: [any time you spank a child, you're putting something up in his brain too] but a child left to himself bringeth his mother to shame" (Prov. 29:15). Do you believe that's true? Leave a child to himself and he will bring shame upon his family. "Correct thy son and he shall give thee rest; yea, he shall give delight unto thy soul" (Prov. 29:17). That's the Word of God.

I'm laying special emphasis upon Christian discipline because this subject receives so little attention. Someone may ask if I mean to say that the fellow who doesn't rule his children well cannot be a good Christian. That is exactly what I mean—Christian parents make their children obey. It may not be necessary for you to resort to the rod. I am saying, do not be afraid to use it when there is no other way. I am saying that restraint and obedience are essential for the growth of Christian character. Love your child; reason with him; show him the right and the wrong, but whip him if all else fails. The Scriptures say exactly that.

In I Timothy, chapter three, God gives the qualifications for a bishop, a pastor of a church and for a deacon. According to the Bible, a bishop will be "One that ruleth well his own house, having his children in subjection with all gravity." There it is stated clearly that no matter how sound his doctrine, how fervent his spirit, how clean his life, no man is fit to be an officer of the church unless he has his children in hand and in subjection. That's what Scripture says.

I was sitting in the home of a preacher and his wife. Their son Jimmy came into the room where we were talking and the father said, "Jimmy, will you kindly go shut the door for Daddy?" Jimmy began to get red: he glared and stamped his foot. "I won't," he said.

"Please, won't you, Jimmy, just for Daddy, please do."

The preacher father begged and pleaded with Jimmy, but the little boy stomped his foot and left the room. Brother, I'd like to have had that boy for five minutes. He'd have gone into the door shutting business for good. He'd shut every door in that community. We need some old-fashioned discipline in the home.

We still haven't discussed all of the verse: "And, ye fathers, provoke not your children to wrath." The great principle of scriptural teaching is example. Children are repercussions of the parents. You show me a bad child and I'll show you that nine times out of ten there is something wrong with the parents. You are an example to your children.

There was a man who always stopped on his way to the office for a drink of whiskey at the corner tavern. There had been a snowfall the night before and on this particular morning he heard something behind him. When he turned around, there was his little seven-year-old boy, stepping as closely as possible in his father's tracks.

"Son what are you doing? You go back home. You'll catch cold."

The little boy said, "I'm just stepping in your tracks, Daddy."

The father went to the corner saloon but something stopped him that morning. He went to his office, but he could still hear: "Stepping in your tracks, Daddy." Then he began to think. "I come home at night drunk; I come home and use profanity. I love my little boy and he loves me; he wants to follow in my steps, but my steps are leading him to hell." The father dropped to his knees and accepted Jesus Christ as Saviour. Then he made this promise, "I'm going home to be an example to my little boy."

To raise a family in this godless age is a tremendous and fearful responsibility before God! You ought to not take it lightly—it is a heavy responsibility.

Treat your children with love and understanding. It isn't always necessary to whip a child. If you have won and deserved the love and respect of your children, a spoken word is often all that is necessary. Do not give harsh commands to your children. And never make a promise to a child if you do not intend to fulfill it.

"Lord, who am I to teach the ways of little children
        day by day,
So prone myself to go astray,
I teach them knowledge but I know how faint the flicker,
How the candles of my knowledge glow,
I teach them power to will and do but only to learn anew
My own great weakness through and through—
But I find my love comes lagging far behind.
Lord, if their guide I still must be,
Oh, let the little children see their teacher
Leaning hard on Thee."

Let your children see Christ in your life. How I thank God for my parents. I remember my mother and father praying. I thought my dad was mighty strict, but as I look back I thank God for every time he punished me. I thank God for every time my father got on his knees in prayer for his boy. My father, with prayer and a hickory stick, led his boy into the ministry of the gospel of Jesus Christ. He was an example of what a Christian father ought to be, and I stand here tonight and pay him tribute.

What about you as a parent, as a dad, as a mother? Scripture says, "Train up a child in the way he shall go and when he is old he will not depart from it." That is the Word of God.

If you train your child; pray for your children and live a Christ-like life before them, God says, "Some day, though they may be wayward now, some day they will come back."

Tonight you may not be a believer in Jesus. You may act, talk and look as though you are a child of God, but you're not sure that you are. You know it is wonderful to have God for a heavenly Father and to know that heaven is our home. There will be no tears or sorrow in that home.

We sing "There's no place like home." God says that some day we're going to an eternal home to spend eternity with Him. "I go to prepare a place for you," said Jesus. "I am building mansions in the sky. A home for eternity." Sometimes I get tired and discouraged down here. Fears come and burdens are heavy. I'm looking forward to getting home. What about you? It's a glorious home in the sky. With palaces of ivory, gates of pearl, streets of transparent gold. Where there are no tears, no suffering and no burdens. There shall be no night there because the Lord is the sun and moon thereof. Are you going to be there? I'm looking forward to it. How am I going? Not because I prepared to or earned my way, but because the Lord Jesus Christ on the cross of Calvary died for my sins. What about you?

H. C. Morrison went to Africa. He went with one purpose—to lead souls to Christ. As a missionary he labored and suffered for Christ in Africa. When he started home, Teddy Roosevelt was on the same boat. Roosevelt had been in Africa hunting lions. As the ship reached New York harbor, it seemed that all of New York had turned out to welcome Teddy Roosevelt. Ships were blowing their horns, the tugboats were tooting their whistles, bands and the mayor were there. H. C. Morrison said, "Broken in body, I stood on board that ship, the loneliest man in the word. I had been in Africa slaving for Jesus Christ and not a person in that whole crowd to welcome me home." Then he said, "Suddenly that scene in New York faded and I said to myself, 'Why should I be worried? I'm not home yet.'"

In his imagination he saw heaven's gates; he heard the trumpets
blow, the band play, the orchestras of heaven, and the angelic
chorus. He saw the gates flung open and Gabriel shouted, "Open
the gates, H. C. Morrison is coming home." The angels put
new robes on him and together they walked down those golden
streets. Then Morrison came to the Lord Jesus sitting on the
throne. The Lord stepped down from His throne and greeted
him with open arms, saying, "Welcome home, Henry, we've
been waiting a long time for you."

Is heaven your home tonight?

How To Be Filled With The Spirit

THE SUBJECT discussed in this message is extremely controversial—there are many different opinions. I am going to try to stay off controversial points. The very fact that some of us believe one thing and some another does not do away with the fact that God says, "Be ye filled with the Spirit." I believe this is the greatest need of the Church of Jesus Christ today.

Everywhere I go I find that God's people lack something. God's people are hungry for something; God's people are thirsty for something. I find among professing Christians a great need and lack, a feeling of insecurity, and defeat in their Christian lives. Tonight I believe we are going to put our fingers on the reason why so many of us are living lives of defeat. Many of us say that our Christian experience is not all that we expected. We have an oft-recurring defeat in our lives and, as a result, across the country from coast to coast there are hundreds of Christian people hungry for something they do not have. There seems to be little growth in our lives. Instead of going from victory to victory, we are going from defeat to defeat. We have no joy; we have no thrill; it is not exciting. The Christian life is not as glorious and wonderful an adventure as we thought it was going to be. Some of us are living only as charred embers of the flaming devotion we had when we came to Christ.

This scripture says, "Be ye filled with the Spirit." That is not optional—that is a command. The first part of the verse says, "Be not drunk with wine." I was preaching in a church down South some time ago. A deacon came in drunk one Sunday morning. The church had a congregational meeting and excommunicated him. They should have. I asked the pastor, "Does every deacon come every Sunday filled with the Spirit?" He said, "No." I said, "Did you ever kick them out?"

He said, "No." I said, "Did you know that the same scripture that says, 'Be not drunk with wine,' also says, 'Be ye filled with the Spirit?'" That statement is not just good advice; it is not just a pat on the shoulder from God and His saying, "I hope you are filled with the Spirit." God Almighty said, "Be ye filled with the Spirit."

I ask you tonight, "Are you filled with the Spirit?" You Christians, are you filled with the Spirit? If not, you are sinning against God. You have no victory in your life. There is no joy, no thrill and no brilliancy in your life tonight unless you are filled with the Spirit.

Now, turn with me to Ezekiel 37:4. Here we find a good illustration of people that are without the fulness of the Spirit:

> "Again he said unto me, Prophecy upon these bones, and say unto them, O ye dry bones, hear the word of the Lord. Thus saith the Lord God unto these bones; Behold, I will cause breath to enter into you, and ye shall live: And I will lay sinews upon you, and will bring up flesh upon you, and cover you with skin, and put breath in you, and ye shall live; and ye shall know that I am the Lord. So I prophesied as I was commanded: and as I prophesied, there was a noise, and behold a shaking, and the bones came together, bone to his bone. And when I beheld, lo, the sinews and the flesh came up upon them, and the skin covered them above: but there was no breath in them."

Did you know that that is the picture of a vast majority of the members of the Church of Jesus Christ today? The bones are in place, the organization is well oiled, and the machinery is running fast. We have our chairmen, our committees, and all of the organization we need, but there is so little breath in us that we can't even take a breath. Bone upon bone, all the sinews and flesh muscles in place, blood vessels, eyes, hands, feet, ears, nose, hair, but no breath! That to me is the picture of thousands of Christians tonight. We have everything except the breath of God. We have everything except the fulness of the Holy Spirit.

Then if you turn to the first chapters of Matthew and the first chapters of Luke, you will find the story of the birth of Jesus. I want you to think reverently of this fact—the womb of Mary was barren until the Holy Spirit conceived the young child Jesus. That womb was absolutely dependent upon the Holy Spirit. So today our lives are barren and fruitless without the power and the fulness of the Holy Spirit.

Then I want you to see something else. I want you to see 120 people banded together. They are in an upper room, afraid and nervous. They are trembling because many people are milling around outside waiting to persecute and kill them. Suddenly the Holy Spirit comes in all of His fulness and these people go out to turn the world upside down! They were powerless—they had no power until the Holy Spirit came upon them. "Ye shall receive power, after that the Holy Spirit is come upon you" (Acts 1:8).

The Church today is powerless. We are gathering for our prayer meetings, church services and Sunday school conventions. Committees meet; Bible classes are conducted; Bible schools are carried on, but we have no power because we do not have the Spirit of God in power and in fulness in our lives. The Bible says, "Be ye filled with the Spirit."

Remember the young fellow in the sixth chapter of II Kings? He was going out to chop down trees. As he was chopping, the axe head fell off and into the stream. Now this young fellow didn't take the old axe handle and keep on chopping. He went to Elisha, and said, "Elisha, I have lost the axe head." And Elisha went back with him, took a stick and held it over the water and "the iron did swim."

Do you know what a lot of us are doing? A long time ago we lost the axe head, but we are still chopping with the handle. We are trying to chop down the trees, trying to win souls, trying to live a Christian life, trying to produce the fruit of the Spirit with the old axe handle and the head is gone. I am praying that the axe head will swim, and I am praying that the axe head will be back on the handle in your life before you leave this place tonight.

Are you filled with the Spirit? I am persuaded that our desperate need tonight is not a new organization nor a new movement, nor a new method—we have enough of those. I believe the greatest need tonight is that our men and women who profess the name of Jesus Christ be filled with the Spirit. Are you filled with the Spirit? I do not believe it is possible to teach a Sunday school class with power unless you are filled with the Spirit. It is not possible to preach with power unless you are filled with the Spirit. It is not possible to reproduce the life of Christ daily unless you are filled with the Spirit. "Be ye filled with the Spirit!"

Now turn to Galatians 5:22. "But the fruit of the Spirit is love, joy, temperance, longsuffering, gentleness, goodness, faith, meekness, temperance." That is the fruit of the Spirit, and you and I are doing our very best to produce that fruit. For a long time I tried. I tried, and tried, and tried. I struggled and struggled and struggled—I did like Paul in the seventh chapter of Romans. I wanted to do good, but evil was present with me—there was a raging conflict all the time and I had no victory. You know why? Because the fruit of the Spirit can't be worked up. It can't be brought about by men or women in their own strength. It is by the power of the Lord Jesus Christ in the form of the Holy Spirit which He has given us that produces this fruit. It is impossible to produce the Christ-life without the fulness of the Holy Spirit. It cannot be done! You may try to do so. You may work your fingernails off; you may work day and night to try to produce love, but you will never produce genuine love without the Spirit of God. You may try to have peace and try to be calm under all circumstances, but you will never produce peace without the Spirit of God. You may cry and plead to have joy in your life; you may run from pleasure to pleasure; attend many social events; read books which you believe will bring joy; but you will never have real joy outside the Spirit of the living God because He alone produces joy. You may want patience and say, "Lord, control my tongue. Lord, I don't want to fly off the handle. I don't want to tell people where to get off." You will never have victory until the Holy Spirit gives you the victory.

In addition to trying to produce the fruit of the Spirit, do you know the second thing we are trying to do? We are attempting to have supernatural power without the fulness of the Spirit. Jesus said, "All power is given unto me in heaven and in earth. Go ye therefore, and teach all nations" (Matt. 28:18, 19). In other words, we are sent forth to do a supernatural job, and don't think it is not a "super-natural" job. Winning a man to Jesus Christ cannot be done apart from the Spirit of God. It is the Spirit of God that does the convicting; the Spirit of God does the regenerating; He does the pleading. It is the Spirit of God that brings a man to accept Christ, not you. You are only a witness and a channel. We are trying to do the work of the Holy Spirit without supernatural power. It cannot be done!

When God told us to go and preach the gospel to every creature and to evangelize the world, He provided supernatural power for us. That power is given to us by the Holy Spirit. It is available to every one of us. It is more powerful than atomic power or TNT. It is more potent than any explosive ever made by man. God said that "we shall have power after that the Holy Spirit comes upon us." Do you know anything of the power of the Holy Spirit?

You may say, "I want to be filled, I want joy in my life. I want to produce the fruit of the Spirit in my life. I want victory in my life. I don't want to live this up and down life. I don't want to be up one day and down the next day. I don't want this great conflict inside of me all the time. I want victory in my life. I want to live on the mountain-top, above the clouds.

I want to live up on the sunlit peak of God's grace and love. I want to shine for Christ as one of those brilliant, radiant Christians." Do you? Do you really mean it? Are you hungry and thirsty to produce the fruit of the Spirit. Do you really want to have power in witnessing? Do you want to see people saved when you speak to them? Are you hungry tonight to have inner peace and joy? Do you want your conflicts and frustrations settled? Are you hungry tonight to have the chains, bonds and fetters of evil habits broken? What would it mean to you to have daily consistent victory day in and day out? Perhaps the prayer meeting isn't very attractive to you, and, if you admit it, you have to fight to read your Bible, so you don't read it very much.

If you really want to change and be filled with the Holy Spirit you can, but it costs something. There is a price. Are you willing to pay for an abundant life, for a thrilling, exciting adventure? If so, I guarantee to you on the authority of the Word of God that it is available to every man, woman, boy and girl in Christ.

What is the first step? The first step is cleansing from sin. God has not called us to uncleanness, but unto holiness. Scripture says, "Create in me a clean heart." The Bible tells us, "The blood of Jesus Christ cleanseth us." That word "cleanseth" means "continue to cleanse" from every sin. Then we read, "If we confess our sins, he is faithful and just to forgive us our sins, and to cleanse us from all unrighteousness." This is God's remedy for your sins.

The Psalmist said, "If I regard iniquity in my heart, the Lord will not hear me" (Ps. 66:18.) Now the first thing you have to do is confess your sins before God. Don't tell Him only some of the things you've done wrong; you have to be honest with God.

What kind of sins need confessing? Well, there are the sins of omission: the first one is ingratitude. We have rain once in awhile in California; sometimes sunshine, but I wonder how often we stop to thank God for rain and sunlight. Our thanklessness is a sin in the sight of God and we should confess it.

The second sin of omission is a lack of love for God. Now listen, God is a jealous God. How would you like it if your wife or husband gave you only as little time as you give God? Suppose your husband or wife were too busy with outside interests to be faithful to you. When we say God is a jealous God, we mean that He wants our full attention; when we are unfaithful to Him, it is sin.

The third sin of omission is neglect of the Word. The Bible says to study the Word, and to desire the sincere milk of the Word that ye may grow thereby. How long since you read your Bible? I used to be a pastor of a church and I remember that one time I went to call on one of the members of my church. Of course, like all good pastors, I sort of took my time going up the walk so they would have plenty of time to see me and get ready. Then I rang the doorbell and sort of peeked in the window which was right next to the door. I saw the most awful commotion—these people were putting a deck of cards away and they were getting out the old family Bible, dusting it off to make me believe that they had been reading the Bible. Did you ever do that? I don't think anybody in Los Angeles ever did, but listen, we have so little Bible reading, so little Bible study that it is a sin against God.

The fourth sin is unbelief. Did you know that every time you don't believe God, you are really saying, "God, You are a liar." God says, "I will answer your prayer." "Well, Lord, I didn't think You'd do it," we say. Our faith is often like that of the woman who prayed for the mountain to be removed into the sea, and she got up the next morning, looked out and said, "Well, I didn't think it would be." We pray for revival and if God does not send it, we say, "I didn't think we'd have revival, anyway." We pray that God will supply our need. Maybe we become impatient and say, "I have been doubting all the time that He would." We have no faith! We are saying, "Lord, You are a liar, You are a liar."

Suppose your little boy wanted you to give him a dollar. He came to ask for it continually, but always said, "Daddy, you are a great big old liar, you're just a liar, you've lied." Would you be inclined to reward his unbelief in you by giving him a dollar? I don't think so.

The next sin is neglect of prayer. How long has it been since you really spent time with God privately? Don't think that you can grow in your Christian life without prayer; lack of prayer is sin. We need to confess our prayerlessness.

The sixth sin is failure to attend church services. The Bible says, "Neglect not the assembling of yourselves together." For some of us it's been a long time since we attended church regularly. This is a sin against Almighty God.

Then we lack a passion for souls — a burning desire to lead unbelievers to know Christ. Passion is intense and deep. Do you feel that way about those afar from God?

Other sins of omission are neglect of family duty — we forget the family altar; our hospitality is cold; we refuse to deny ourselves; all these are sins.

Next there are sins of commission that we need to confess. These include the sins of worldliness, pride, envy, a bitter spirit, holding a grudge, slander and gossiping, lying, cheating, hypocrisy, robbing God, temper, malice. All these things God says have to be confessed; put away and given up for good. Maybe you have confessed sins such as these, but you have not renounced them. The Bible says not only to confess, but to forsake and God will have mercy. There are many of us who come before the Lord: confess a sin, but go back to commit it the next day. Then we come again to confess it to the Lord and think we are forgiven. Afterwards we repeat the sin again. That is not confession. Genuine Spirit-directed confession means renunciation as well. Both Saul and Judas admitted that they were sinners. These men admitted sin, but they did not renounce it. Have you renounced your sin, or did you just say, "Now, Lord, forgive my sins," only to repeat them again? That prayer doesn't get any higher than the ceiling. God says, we must be cleansed of all our sins. When you confess your sin, God forgives and cleanses. He washes sin away. His Word says, "If we confess our sins [talking to Christians], he is faithful and just to forgive us our sins, and to cleanse us from all unrighteousness" (I John 1:9). I am glad I can tell you tonight that anyone can know his sins are forgiven; that he is cleansed and that God remembers sin against that individual no more.

You say, "But I don't feel like it." Forget your feelings for a moment and take God's Word. We rely too much on feelings. My feelings change every day. One day I eat a green apple and get sick and I feel bad. The next day I sleep about ten or twelve hours and I feel good; I am ready to whip the world. Then the next day I may feel bad again. Suppose I were going on my feelings. I would be down one day and up the next. It is not feeling that proves forgiveness. It is the Word of Almighty God. When we confess our sin, God Almighty says He forgives! The Devil is the one who keeps your sin fresh in your mind. He will say, "Well, you confessed it, but it is still bothering you." He will do his best to worry you. He likes to see you become discouraged so you will go back and commit sin again because you are discouraged. Don't let Satan defeat you on that point! Believe God! When God says sins are forgiven, they are forgiven; they are buried in the sea and God remembers them against you no more. Take it by faith for it is a matter of faith.

After we have confessed our sins, we need the second step — consecration. "Know ye not, that to whom ye yield yourselves servants to obey, his servants ye are to whom ye obey; whether of sin unto death, or of obedience unto righteousness?" (Rom. 6:16). "Neither yield ye your members as instruments of unrighteousness unto sin: but yield yourselves unto God, as those that are alive from the dead, and your members as instruments of righteousness unto God" (Rom. 6:13).

Paul says, "I beseech you therefore, brethren, by the mercies of God, that ye present your bodies a living sacrifice, holy, acceptable unto God, which is your reasonable service" (Rom. 12:1). Now, what is consecration? Consecration is simply surrender, yielding. If someone should ask me to sum up in one word what victorious living is, I would say "yielding." I mean yielding all to God, letting God have His way in every phase of your life. I mean everything — 100 per cent.

A young man wanted to rent his house. Another fellow said, "I'd like to rent the house. There is a housing shortage and I have had a pretty tough time."

"All right," said the first man, "I will rent you the house, but there is one room I am going to keep for myself.

"What are you going to keep in that room?" asked the other fellow.

"Well, I've got a pet tiger I am going to keep in there."

You may smile at this, but that is what some of us have said to God. "Lord, You can have every bit of my house. Lord, You can have the bedroom, You can have the living room, and, Lord, You can have the dining room, the pantry, and the closet. But, Lord, please let me keep the kitchen and the icebox. I've got something there I want just for myself." That's what we say to the Lord. "Lord, You can have every part of my personality, and You can have everything, but, Lord, there is just one little thing I want to keep for myself. Lord, it is a harmless little thing. It doesn't mean much. I know You won't mind. Won't You let me keep it?" We go on trying to keep some secret sin; we never yield it and never surrender it; and we never know what real consecration is. Are you holding back on God?

A young woman came to a friend of mine and said, "Dr. Bob, there is something wrong in my life. I am defeated, Dr. Bob. I wish I had some victory in my life, but it seems like I just can't get it." She loved to play the violin. She was the best violinist in the school. But Dr. Bob said, "Mary, before you can have victory, you have to surrender that violin to the Lord."

"Oh, but Dr. Bob, you don't understand. I have studied this all my life. It is my life! It's everything to me, and it — it's the Lord's."

"I know. But that is your difficulty. Your violin, even though it is used for God, means more to you than God does."

"I'm sorry," she said, "but I just can't give God the violin."

She went away and was in misery. Mary dropped out of school and for one year she lived a life of frustration and conflict. She had no peace, no power, no joy. Then one morning, about two o'clock, she took her violin and said, "Oh, Lord, here it is." The most wonderful peace came over her. The Lord didn't take her violin at all; she kept right on playing. He just wanted first place. Now Mary realizes that her violin is secondary; her devotion belongs first to God.

Sometimes we let little things stand in the way. You may let your family stand between you and God. We let love of *things* prevent our love of *God*. We are holding back on God and fail to consecrate ourselves to Him.

You have heard about the little girl who reached for something at the bottom of a vase. She couldn't get her hand out again. Now this vase cost a great deal. The father and mother worked with the little girl for a long time. Then they called the doctor who said there was nothing to do to get that little hand out of the vase except to break the vase. Finally the father said, "Honey, won't you please just relax your hand and see if Daddy can't get it out this time." The little girl said, "But, Daddy, if I do, I'll lose the penny I am holding onto." She let loose of the penny when he promised to give her more than one penny, and out the hand came.

Some or us are holding onto a little old penny while God is saying, "Let loose of the penny, and I'll give you a thousand

pennies. Just let loose." Let loose of the little old pennies in
your life. Let go of those things that are holding you back
from complete surrender.

You may say, "What does that have to do with the filling
of the Holy Spirit?" Turn to this passage of Scripture:

> "When the unclean spirit is gone out of a man, he walk-
> eth through dry places, seeking rest; and finding none, he
> saith, I will return unto my house whence I came out. And
> when he cometh, he findeth it swept and garnished. Then
> goeth he, and taketh to him seven other spirits more wicked
> than himself; and they enter in, and dwell there; and the last
> state of that man is worse than the first" (Luke 11:24).

Here is the story I want you to get. See this house where
the evil spirit has been cast out. The house has been swept
clean of all cobwebs and dirt; it is clean.

When you are yielded and your sins are confessed, you
are in a dangerous position. Do you know why? Because
the old evil spirit that left the house is going to get seven
others worse than himself, and then he is going to look in the
window of your house. If he finds nothing there — the place
is still empty — he is going to open the door and come in.
Your state will then be far worse than it ever was before.
You will have seven demons instead of one; seven sins instead
of one; seven troubles instead of one; seven heartaches instead
of one; seven tragedies instead of one.

But if you cleanse your heart of sin and it is then filled
with the Holy Spirit, it is an entirely different matter. The
evil spirit can't get in.

You say, "That's what I want." Well, first of all, you are
indwelt by the Spirit. Scripture says, "Know ye not that ye
are the temple of God, and that the Spirit of God dwelleth
in you?" (I Cor. 3:16). Acts 10:45 says that the Holy Spirit
is a gift from God. God says you are indwelt right now by
the Spirit if you are a Christian. I am not talking about fulness;

I am talking about indwelling. The Spirit of God lives in you right now. You say, "But I don't feel like it." Forget feelings! It's faith in God's Word. God says that the moment I accept Christ, I am indwelt by the Spirit of God.

Now, how can I be filled with the Spirit? "As ye have therefore received Christ Jesus the Lord, so walk ye in him" (Col. 2:6). How did I receive Him? Did I work for it? No! Did I cry and beg? No. One day, by faith, I received Jesus, and so I receive the fulness of the Spirit of God by faith. By faith I can know that I am filled with the Spirit. If I have been cleansed from sin and absolutely yielded to God with nothing held back, then by faith I can claim the fulness of the Holy Spirit in my life.

I didn't work for salvation, did I? "For by grace are ye saved through faith; and that not of yourselves: it is the gift of God" (Eph. 2:8). Some people join the church in an attempt to be saved. Others are baptized, believing that this means salvation. You ought to be baptized and you ought to join the church, but *after* you accept Christ as Saviour. Joining the church or being baptized will not save you. Our works and our righteousness are as filthy rags in the sight of Almighty God. It is by faith, and only faith, in the cleansing power of the blood of the Lord Jesus Christ, shed on Calvary, that I am saved.

When I first accepted Christ, I felt as though I were walking on air. It was wonderful to know Christ and to be saved. I was so excited I couldn't wait until I got home to tell everybody. But feelings do not mean that I was saved. I might not have had that much feeling, because each one of us has a different emotional make-up. But by faith I knew I was saved. God said, "if thou shalt confess with thy mouth the Lord Jesus, and shalt believe in thine heart that God hath raised him from the dead, thou shalt be saved" (Rom. 10:9). I knew I was saved because God Almighty said so.

Then how can I know that I am filled with the Spirit? First, I have courage to witness. Read the book of Acts. You will find there these words twenty-six times: "They spoke boldly the word of the Lord." When you are filled with the Spirit, you are witnessing for Christ all the time — in the shop, in the factory, on the street car, in the plane; wherever you are, you are witnessing for Christ and telling others about Him. People may laugh at you and sneer at your beliefs. They may think you are a crazy fanatic, but it makes no difference. In spite of persecution, mocking and sneering, you are witnessing daily for the Lord Jesus Christ.

The second proof of the fulness of the Spirit is seen in producing the fruit of the Spirit. "But the fruit of the Spirit is love, joy, peace, longsuffering, gentleness, goodness, faith, meekness, temperance" (Gal. 5:22, 23). The fruit of the Spirit — that word is singular and it means in one cluster, one fruit. Nine parts to it, but still one fruit. You cannot have love without joy; you cannot have joy without peace; you cannot have peace without temperance; and you cannot have temperance without meekness. All of these fruits are produced as one. If you have genuine peace, you will have genuine love. If you have genuine love, you will have genuine meekness. All of them go together because they are produced by the Spirit of God. How do I know that I am filled with His Spirit? I know it if I am producing the fruit of the Spirit. How do you know that you are filled? Because you are witnessing for Christ and producing the fruit of the Spirit.

The third proof is the place Christ has in your life. Does He have first place? Is He pre-eminent? The Holy Spirit always exalts and magnifies the Lord Jesus. He came not to speak of Himself but to speak of Christ. If I see Christ living in a man, and I see that man radiating Christ; producing the fruit of the Spirit; witnessing for Christ; and Christ is exalted and magnified in his life, I can be very sure that this Christian knows something of the fulness of the Spirit.

Think again of the fruit of the Spirit. First is love. That means you never gossip; you never talk about people; you are always sweet, gracious, kind, tender-hearted. You are never angry; never jealous of anyone. This verse says that you have peace, joy, and that you are patient with everybody. You have faith. You are honest and kind. All of these things make up the fruit of the Spirit.

If a man is walking in the power of the Holy Spirit and has the fulness of the Spirit, he has power to witness. He produces the fruit of the Spirit and Christ has first place in his life. Are you filled with the Spirit?

I want to say something very dangerous. Did you know that it is possible to work for the Lord and live an exemplary life without being filled with the Spirit? It says concerning the Corinthians that they came behind in no gift (I Cor. 1:5-7). But Paul called them carnal Christians. (I Cor. 3:1). This means that I can have the gift of an evangelist. I can get up and preach and still not be filled with the Spirit. I shall preach without power and my preachings will be as sounding brass and tinkling cymbal. You may have the gift of teaching a Sunday school class. You can have the gift without being filled with the Spirit. Because you can get up and talk or teach the Bible does not necessarily mean that you are filled with the Spirit. What an awful thing that is!

I have asked God if there were ever a day when I should stand in the pulpit without knowing the fulness and anointing of the Spirit of God and should not preach with compassion and fire, I want God to take me home to heaven. I don't want to live. I don't ever want to stand in the pulpit and preach without the power of the Holy Spirit. It's a dangerous thing.

Some of you may have the gift of administration. Maybe you are an administrator for God — that's a gift of the Spirit. You may have another gift: you may have the gift of prophecy. You may have any of the other spiritual gifts mentioned in I

Corinthians 12. You can have all of them and still not be filled with the Spirit! I ask you pastors tonight, I ask myself, I ask you Sunday school teachers, you Christian workers, you church members — are you filled with the Holy Spirit?

That's the reason we don't have revival in this country. That's the reason Los Angeles isn't moved to turn to God. Members of the church of Jesus Christ know so little of the fulness of the Spirit of God. Do you know why we know so little? Because we are not ready to pay the price. The price of confession, yielding and faith in the Word of Almighty God. Are you filled tonight? Are you producing the fruit? Are you witnessing in the power of the Spirit?

John Hyde was on his way to a mission station in India. While he was on board ship, he received this telegram: "Are you filled with the Spirit?" He was known as a great Presbyterian preacher and his first reaction, as he crumpled the telegram and put it in his pocket, was "The audacity of somebody sending me a telegram, asking me if I am filled with the Spirit. Of course I am, I am a missionary!" Then he stalked to his stateroom. But somehow the Spirit of God spoke to him. He pulled the telegram from his pocket and read it again. He got down on his knees and yielded himself completely to the Lord. He surrendered everything and claimed by faith the power of the Holy Spirit in his life. John Hyde went to India and a great revival came. He went from India to Korea. In 1902 and 1905 they had the great Korean revival. It started among the Presbyterian missionaries of Korea and swept Korea because one man was filled with the Holy Spirit.

Jonathan Goforth, way up in Manchuria, heard about it. He came down; saw the revival and received knowledge of the Spirit-filled life. Then Goforth went back to Manchuria, and one of the greatest revivals of all time broke out in Manchuria. Three great revivals because one man was filled with the Spirit.

What could take place in the city of Los Angeles if you people here tonight could know something of the fulness and the power of the Spirit of God? Are you willing to pay the price? Revival will come when God's people are ready to pay the price!

Prepare To Meet Thy God!

"Also Amaziah said unto Amos, O thou seer, go, flee thee away into the land of Judah, and there eat bread, and prophesy there: But prophesy not again any more at Bethel: for it is the king's chapel, and it is the king's court.

"Then answered Amos, and said to Amaziah, I was no prophet, neither was I a prophet's son: but I was an herdsman, and a gatherer of sycamore fruit: And the Lord took me as I followed the flock, and the Lord said unto me, Go, prophesy unto my people Israel.

"Now therefore hear thou the word of the Lord: Thou sayest, Prophesy not against Israel, and drop not thy word against the house of Isaac. Therefore thus saith the Lord; Thy wife shall be an harlot in the city, and thy sons and thy daughters shall fall by the sword, and thy land shall be divided by line; and thou shalt die in a polluted land: and Israel shall surely go into capitivity forth of his land" (Amos 7:12-17).

TODAY Europe, the Far East and America have heard the radio story of Mr. Truman's Friday (Sept. 23, 1949) morning message. This Nation now knows that Russia has the atomic bomb! Mr. Truman said in yesterday's press conference that we must be prepared for *any* eventuality at *any* hour. Today Moscow announced that Russia has been piling up bombs for over two years and three gigantic plants have been turning out atomic bombs! Radio warnings have been issued from behind the Iron Curtain, and our own President declares, "We must be prepared!"

I am persuaded that time is desperately short. I am persuaded that this thing, happening in the world today, should drive America to repentance of sin and to faith in Jesus Christ. I am also convinced that the only hope of preserving our way of life, the only hope of preserving our present culture, is an old-fashioned, heaven-sent revival. We are praying that during these days it will begin in the city of Los Angeles. I believe that if Los Angeles had a revival, that revival would sweep the nation and the world! Because Los Angeles sets so many of the world's standards, and the world looks to Los Angeles for so much, if Los Angeles were to be bathed by the power of God and were to be moved by a revival, the entire world might be influenced. Let's pray that God may send us a revival of that kind.

Mr. Truman, speaking of this week's events, said that we must be prepared. Go back with me 800 years before Christ, for I want you to see something happening in that day. I want you to see the southern kingdom, called Judah, and the northern kingdom that we call Israel. See these two mighty kingdoms as they existed at the same time. But I want you to see something radically wrong. Notice that they have wandered far away from God, from the God of their fathers. They have denied the Lord God of Israel and have turned their backs upon God's prophets. I want you to see God as He reaches down into the southern kingdom and chooses a man by the name of Isaiah, and He says, "Isaiah, I want you to go up and down the land, and I want you to preach My message. Tell the people of Judah to prepare to meet God before it is too late. Tell them to turn from their wickedness, from their godlessness, from worshipping Baal, and to turn to Me before it is too late."

At the same time God was calling another young man from the northern kingdom. That young man was Amos. I want you to see Amos as he follows his flock of sheep. God came to Amos and said, "Amos, I want you to go to the king's court. I want you to go to the king's chapel and tell the king, tell all the countries and tell the nation of Israel to repent of sin and prepare to meet God before it is too late."

Amos said, "But, Lord, I'm no preacher! I'm just a herdsman, I'm a gatherer of sycamore fruit. And, Lord, I don't know anything about preaching."

Then God said, "Amos, I'll give you the courage; I'll give you the strength; I'll give you the message; I'll open the door."

So Amos left his flock and went to the house, and put on the best outfit that he had and started down the narrow, crooked, dusty road toward Bethel to the king's chapel. I want you to see Amos, the simple shepherd and gatherer of sycamore fruit as he trudges along to the king's court.

Let me tell you something: when God gets ready to shake America, He may not take the Ph.D. and the D.D. God may choose a country boy. God may choose a shoe salesman like He did D. L. Moody. He may choose a baseball player like He did Billy Sunday. God is not limited to the limitations we give Him. God may choose the man that no one knows, a little nobody, to shake America for Jesus Christ in this day, and I pray that He would! We need a voice that sounds forth, "Thus saith the Lord."

Amos was on his way to tell the king to repent of his sin and to prepare to meet God. I want you to see him when he is still a long way off. Perhaps Amaziah, the priest of the golden calf at Bethel, is dressed in all of his robes and stands at the king's chapel. He looks way down the road and says, "I wonder who that fellow is?" Then as Amos draws closer he says, "Why, look at that hill-billy yonder. Wonder why he wants to see the king? We'll have a little fun with this boy." We may well imagine that a conversation such as this took place. Amaziah says, "Hill-billy, what do you want?"

Amos says, "I want to see the king."

"So you want to see the king, eh? Well, everybody wants to see the king. Do you have an appointment?"

"No, I don't have an appointment except the Lord God told me to come deliver a message to the king of Israel."

"Oh, so you want to preach, eh? Well, if you want to preach, you go back to the hill-billies and preach. This is the king's court, and we don't allow any hill-billy preachers up here telling the king what to do."

But Amos, with his faith and obedience to God, pushes Amaziah out of the way and stalks right into where the king holds court. I want you to see the soldiers as they reach for their swords; the guards as they pick up their javelins ready to throw at Amos standing in the king's court. But there is something about his walk, the snap of his eyes, the set of his jaw and squaring of his shoulders that makes them stop as they see Amos standing, filled with the Holy Spirit, ready to declare God's message to the king of Israel.

The king of Israel says, "What do you want? Speak, my man."

Amos, looking the king squarely in the face, points his finger at the king and says, "Oh, king of Israel, thus saith the Lord," and Amos told him many of the things which were to befall Israel. Then he said, "The Lord God says, 'Prepare to meet thy God.'"

I say to you, the message of the Lord has not changed! The message is still the same—prepare to meet thy God! We had better prepare to meet our God—the day of judgment is coming desperately near! The day of reckoning is coming desperately close! People of Los Angeles, PREPARE TO MEET THY GOD is the message that God has for us tonight!

But I want to talk to you as individuals. I want to talk to you as though you were sitting across from me in front of the hearth. I want to talk to you about preparing right now!

First of all we must prepare for life. We must prepare to meet the issues of life as we find them. No man is prepared to live and to meet the issues of life unless he has Jesus Christ, because Christ is the answer, and the only answer, to all the problems and issues and difficulties of life. We face a number of problems today.

The first problem that we face is the problem of fear. Did you know that there are thousands of people in this great city that are afraid tonight? Hundreds of people are afraid of failure—failure in business, failure in vocation, failure in social circles, failure in society. There are hundreds of people that are afraid of old age. The other day I saw a young man stand in front of a mirror; reach up in his hair and pull something out. Then I said, "What are you doing?" He said, "I'm pulling out a gray hair. I hate to get old." This is an age in which the accent is on youth and everybody is trying to stay young.

There are other people who are afraid of war, afraid of atomic bombs, fearful as they go to bed at night. That is particularly true in Europe tonight. I heard a radio commentator talking from London, saying that fear has gripped the hearts of millions of people in Europe. They are going to bed tonight trembling because they feel that we are on the verge of a third World War—a war which could sweep civilization back into the Middle Ages.

There are other thousands who are afraid of death. They don't know exactly what lies beyond this life. When they come face to face with death, whether it be a heart attack, a motor car accident, or a hospital experience—they are afraid! They are afraid they are going to die!

Still other people are afraid of failing health. They do everything to keep their health, alarmed lest some crippling ailment or disabling illness come to them.

Second to the problem of fear is the problem of sex. Sex has gotten out of control. Sex is out of kilter. Sex is overplayed and emphasized until we forget that this mighty, powerful creative energy is from the Lord.

The third problem is non-constructive habits. Habits which we don't know how to break. This week a young man came to me and said, "I'd give anything in the world if I could break the power of drink in my life! I am an alcoholic at the age of 26, and I can't break this power in my life."

I said, "Young man, I know the Person Who can break it for you, and that Person is Jesus Christ."

Then there is the dope addict. We face a thousand and one habits and we have no solution outside of Jesus Christ.

There are ethical problems. We have something way down inside of us that says, "This is wrong, and that is right." We face tremendous problems in realms of philosophy that have no answer outside of Jesus Christ. Where do we come from? Why are we here? Where are we going? All of these questions have no answer outside the Lord Jesus Christ.

And then in this country, particularly in this town, we face the problem of boredom. You say, "Well, that's not true." I wish you could read the hundreds of letters that I received when I spoke on the subject of being bored with life. Thousands of people tonight are bored with living. That is the reason we have many suicides. Bored with life! A young movie star right here in Hollywood committed suicide last year because she was bored with life. She had lived to the ripe old age of twenty-nine, and there was nothing left to live for, so she committed suicide. Lots of people feel that way tonight.

Suppose I went to a certain home that was locked—every door in the home locked, every drawer locked, every closet locked—and I tried many keys but none fitted. Then I took the last key I had and that key opened the front door, the kitchen door, the pantry door, the closet door, the bedroom door and every room in the house. How long do you think it would take me to be persuaded that that was the master key?

Take all the problems that you and I face. Then take the key of philosophy, the key of science, the key of psychology, or any of these other keys, and try to unlock these doors. Perhaps you will find that a few may open with these keys, but most of them will stay tightly closed until you try the Lord Jesus Christ. Then take Him and unlock every door in your house, every problem that you face, for you will find that He is the Master Key! He has unlocked every problem in your life. I don't care what the problem is, I don't care what burden you bear tonight—the Lord Jesus can lift it! Cast all your care upon

Him for He careth for us. Nothing is too hard for our God! Every problem that you face in business, health problems, problems that you face in everyday life—Jesus Christ the Son of God has an answer if you try Him! You have problems in the home, marital problems, problems that are too intimate to discuss with your nearest friend—Jesus has the answer to those problems!

You have a problem tonight of sin. You say, "I'm not troubled with sin." Then you are the only one in the world outside of Christ who is not troubled with sin, because the Bible says, "All have sinned and come short of the glory of God." The Bible says, "The wages of sin is death," and "The soul that sinneth it shall die." The Bible says, "In sin did my mother conceive me." I was born in sin, and I have the problem of sin to deal with and to face, and the only One that has the answer is the Lord Jesus Christ on the cross of Calvary. There is no answer aside from Him. There is no way of cleansing from sin outside of Christ. "There is none other name under heaven, given among men, whereby we must be saved." The Lord Jesus Christ is the only way!

After we have found a way to live and solve life's problems, we must face the problem of death. God says, "It is appointed unto man once to die." He tells us, "Prepare to meet Me." What happens immediately after death? The moment your heart stops beating, the moment you take your last breath, you stand on the threshold of eternity, face to face with Almighty God! How will it be with your soul in those last few moments before you stand on the other side?

A few months ago I talked to a man in the hospital. He said, "I have lived a godless life. I would give my fortune— half a million dollars just to live one more month, but they tell me that I have to die in the next twenty-four hours." And he sobbed bitter, writhing tears of disappointment.

I talked to a man in England. This man was big, strong and husky. Everything came his way, yet he was afraid to die.

He was afraid because he had lived for the Devil instead of for God.

Prepare to meet God at death! Scripture says, "It is appointed unto man once to die." And it is appointed unto you to die—everyone of us will face the grim reaper, should the Lord Jesus tarry. This grim reaper is no respecter of persons.

When Earl Carol stepped on that plane a couple of summers ago, he never dreamed that it would be the last plane he would ride. He said, "Boys, if anything happens to me, the show must go on." But I believe tonight that if he could stand in his beautiful Hollywood restaurant, he would go to the microphone and shout, "Gentlemen, stop your drinking. Girls, stop your dancing. I have a message from eternity, and here it is— Prepare to meet your God!"

Frank Morgan didn't know he would fall asleep last week, never to awaken. Tonight he is somewhere in eternity. We never know when our hour is come.

Tom Brenneman picked up the telephone, not knowing that it would be his last moment on earth and that he would drop dead with a heart attack, face to face with death unexpectedly.

I ask you, are you prepared to die? Are you sure, if this were your last moment, are you prepared to die? I thank God tonight that I know that I am ready to die. Prepared, not because of what I have done—I deserve to die and I deserve hell— but because of what the Lord Jesus Christ did for me on the cross of Calvary, and because I accepted Him by faith and put my trust in Him. "I know whom I have believed, and am persuaded that he is able to keep that which I have committed unto him against that day" (II Tim. 1:12).

Scripture says, "These things I write unto them that believe on the name of the Son of God that ye may know that ye have eternal life."

The Scriptures say that you can know. I'll tell you the greatest thing in the world—do you know what it is? To walk down the street and know that if you drop dead or are killed,

or if you ride in a plane and the plane crashes, you are ready
to meet God! To know that if an atomic bomb comes, you are
ready to meet God! Let war come, let the bombs fall, let the
bullets fly, let the motor car race across the country, thanks be
unto God for I am ready to meet Him. I have nothing to fear.
When the Lord Jesus was raised from the dead, it was a guarantee that I, too, shall rise from the dead in that day of resurrection or, should He come, I shall meet my Lord in the air.
Are you ready to meet God? Are you sure of it? Are you certain of it?

We are told in the Scriptures to be prepared to meet God
at the Judgment. You say, "You mean that we are going to be
judged?" We sure are! The Scriptures say so. All nature points
to the fact that some day there is going to be a reckoning,
some day there is going to be a settlement, some day the wrong
things are going to be made right. Some day all the Hitlers and
all the Mussolinis and all the Stalins and all the other international tyrants are going to stand before God. Then every knee
shall bow and every tongue shall confess that He is Lord of
lords and King of kings. Each man and woman who has not
accepted Christ will stand at the Great White Throne Judgment
to give an account of what he did with Jesus.

If you have never listened to anything else in your life,
listen to these words. If you never come back, listen to this
scripture. Here is God's Almighty Word. This is God's description of His Judgment Day, a day when every unbeliever
must stand to be judged.

> "And I saw a great white throne, and him that sat on
> it, from whose face the earth and the heaven fled away; and
> there was found no place for them. And I saw the dead,
> small and great, stand before God; and the books were
> opened: and another book was opened, which is the book
> of life: and the dead were judged out of those things which
> were written in the books, according to their works. And
> the sea gave up the dead which were in it; and death and

hell delivered up the dead which were in them: and they were judged every man according to their works. And death and hell were cast into the lake of fire. This is the second death. And whosoever was not found written in the book of life was cast into the lake of fire" (Rev. 20:11-15).

These are the words of the Lord God! They are not my words, not the preacher's words, not your friend's words. These are the words of the Lord God, telling us of every unbeliever's fate.

But there is no judgment for those who believe God and accept His Son. "There is therefore now no condemnation to them that are in Christ Jesus." The judgment of believers took place at the cross of Calvary. God laid upon Jesus the sins of us all, and God judged Him; and Jesus, I speak reverently, went to hell that everyone who accepts Him, need never go. Tonight I stand before God clothed in the righteousness of the Lord Jesus Who was made to be sin, He Who knew no sin. Thanks be unto God, I'll never be cast into the lake of fire and brimstone, and no accusing finger will ever be pointed at me because the Lord Jesus has already borne my sinfulness.

I am talking to every person who has never accepted Christ. Imagine that the time has come when the Judge is speaking. The angels and archangels are in attendance. Time's final drama is about to take place. Skyscrapers have fallen and the wheels of industry have ceased turning; the places of amusement are empty; the cocktail bars are vacant; the theaters have no one in them—all the places of the world are deserted. Motor cars are at a standstill and the beaches are empty. Then God calls for the dead to be brought forth. From the ocean depths where ships were sunk long ago, from graveyards long since forgotten, from the battlefields of the world they come—millions and millions and millions of people. They are crying for the rocks to fall on them, they are crying for the caves to open up and give them a place to hide, but there is no hiding from Him Who sits on the throne. They come before the Lord and they say, "But, Lord, we cast out demons in Your name."

"Depart from Me, ye cursed, I never knew you."

"But, Lord, we were members of the First Church."

"Depart from Me, ye cursed, I never knew you."

"But, Lord, I lived a good life."

"Depart from Me, ye cursed, I never knew you."

"But, Lord, I paid my debts and led a good, respectable life."

"Depart from Me, ye cursed, I never knew you."

The Bible says there will be only one question in that day— what did you do with Jesus? You don't go to hell for drinking liquor, you don't go to hell for using profanity—you go to hell for rejecting Christ! Are you sure that you are ready to meet God? Are you certain that you are saved? If there is the slightest doubt in your mind, you can make sure.

God says, "Prepare to meet God." How do you prepare? "If we confess with our mouths the Lord Jesus and believe in our hearts that God hath raised him from the dead, we shall be saved," the Bible tells us. "But as many as received him, to them gave he power to become the sons of God, even to them that believe on his name" (John 1:12). God says, "Believe on My Son and you will live; and when you die, you will go to heaven."

What a wonderful thing! Are you sure, are you certain? Are you dead sure that if you died tonight, you would go to heaven?

Johnstown, Pennsylvania, had an air of fear and dread a few years ago. The engineers said the great dam which had stood for so many years was going to break in a few hours. The rain had been falling for days, the waters had backed up. When the engineers found a little crack in the dam, they said, "Flee to the hills; go to the mountains; the flood is coming." But there were hundreds of people who said, "Why, those young college students don't know what they're talking about. Talk about a flood coming down and the dam breaking, why that dam has held for years." They stayed on in their places of business, and then, suddenly there was a crash and a roar, and down the valley millions and millions of gallons of water rushed to sweep 300 people to their deaths because they refused to be warned and refused to leave.

I tell you, the words of judgment are about to fall! Repent, and believe, and accept Jesus Christ as your Saviour!

The Resurrection of Jesus Christ

"Moreover, brethren, I declare unto you the gospel which I preached unto you, which also ye have received, and wherein ye stand; By which also ye are saved, if ye keep in memory what I preached unto you, unless ye have believed in vain. For I delivered unto you first of all that which I also received, how that Christ died for our sins according to the scriptures; And that he was buried, and that he rose again the third day, according to the scriptures; And that he was seen of Cephas, then of the twelve: After that, he was seen of above five hundred brethren at once; of whom the greater part remain unto this present, but some are fallen asleep. After that, he was seen of James; then of all the apostles. And last of all he was seen of me also, as of one born out of due time." . . .

"Now if Christ be preached that he rose from the dead, how say some among you that there is no resurrection of the dead? But if there be no resurrection of the dead, then is Christ not risen: And if Christ be not risen, then is our preaching vain, and your faith is also vain. Yea, and we are found false witnesses of God; because we have testified of God that he raised up Christ: whom he raised not up, if so be that the dead rise not. For if the dead rise not, then is not Christ raised: And if Christ be not raised, your faith is vain; ye are yet in your sins. Then they also which are fallen asleep in Christ are perished. If in this life only we have hope in Christ, we are of all men most miserable. But now is Christ risen from the dead, and become the firstfruits of them that slept. For since by man came death, by man came also the resurrection of the dead. For as in Adam all die, even so in Christ shall all be made alive." . . .

"Behold, I shew you a mystery; We shall not all sleep, but we shall all be changed, in a moment, in the twinkling of an eye, at the last trump: for the trumpet shall sound, and the dead shall be raised incorruptible, and we shall be changed. For this corruptible must put on incorruption, and this mortal must put on immortality. So when this corruptible shall have put on incorruption, and this mortal shall have put on immortality, then shall be brought to pass the saying that is written, Death is swallowed up in victory. O death, where is thy sting? O grave, where is thy victory? The sting of death is sin; and the strength of sin is the law. But thanks be to God, which giveth us the victory through our Lord Jesus Christ" (I Cor. 15:1-8; 12-22; 51-57).

TURN BACK in history for a few moments. I want you to see several leaders who have lived and played their part in life. They died, never to rise again. Remember for a moment Pharaoh Shishak who lived two thousand, eight hundred years ago. He was mentioned in the Old Testament; the lord of two Egypts, the founder of a new dynasty, a very boastful and arrogant man. His tomb was opened a few months ago, verifying the Scriptures. They found only a dried and shriveled mummy, for he died and never rose again. Go to the great pyramid built thousands of years ago. It has more than two million three hundred thousand blocks of limestone, and took a hundred thousand workers twenty years to build. But it marks nothing except the failure of a selfish Pharaoh. Today that Pharaoh is still there, never rising from the grave. Charlemagne, who controlled the far-flung Roman Empire, who was crowned king of the Holy Roman Empire on Christmas day 800, is today only a jumble of moldy bones, buried in the dust of his tomb for he never rose again from the grave. Go to the Taj Mahal in India, the most beautiful tomb in all the world, but all that remains of the Mongol emperor and his wife are moldy bones. They died and never rose again. Go to Mt. Vernon; see the grave of the father of our country, George Washington. Stand there at attention, with your hat off, and the tears streaming down your cheeks, honor his memory, but know that George Washington lies in the grave. George Washington, though a great man, father of his country lies buried in a tomb and has never risen from the grave. Or go to Russia to see the body of Lenin. They say that he was embalmed with a fluid that would never let his body decay, and they say that he looks as though he were breathing. There are many people who think that Lenin is the Antichrist and is going to be raised up and will be Satan incarnate. I do not know, but this one thing I do know—Lenin is still in the grave and he has never been raised from the grave. Go to India and see Mahatma Gandhi's burial place. He was one of the greatest men that ever lived, a leader to the masses of India. When Gandhi was shot a few years ago he died and has never risen from the grave.

Every tomb, every burial place of man, whether it be massive as the pyramid or simple as your family plot, speaks of death. Every burial place, every cemetery, every gravestone, every casket, every hearse, are all testimonies of human failure—all prove the scriptural fact that it "is appointed unto man once to die."

The grim reaper calls on the rich and the poor, the black and the white, the red and upon all other colors, nationalities and races. Whether it be in Hollywood or on Skid Row, in a hospital or on Broadway, the grim reaper calls. Whether the name be Franklin Roosevelt, Sam Wood, or Tom Brenneman, it makes no difference. What ever the name, death calls upon all because Scripture says, "It is appointed unto man once to die."

But now, I want you to see something different. I want you to see the life of a Man who came upon the horizon some two thousand years ago. I want you to see something of the life that He lived. Scripture says that He went about doing good; He made the blind see, the deaf hear. He performed miracles, and He taught as one having authority. I wish today that all the ministers in this country could stand behind the sacred desk and preach as having authority. I wish that every man who professes the name of Christ and holds this sacred Book in his hands could back up every word and say, "Thus saith the Lord." I believe it is the message of the hour, the message that needs to be proclaimed from the housetops, in the streets, down on the avenue, in the church, or wherever one might find professing Christians—"Thus saith the Lord." My illustrations don't amount to a hill of beans. What I think about them doesn't amount to a hill of beans. My ideas about philosophy, politics, or world events mean absolutely nothing. I believe that today men and women are hungry to hear "Thus saith the Lord." Today people want to hear what is on the pages of this Book. They want to know what God has to say. They want to know what the Bible says. Night after night in this campaign I have been trying, to the best of my ability, to tell you what God says instead of what man says. Instead of what philosophers or politicians say about world events, I have been trying to tell you what the Scriptures say.

Jesus spoke as a man having authority. Jesus stood up and spoke as the Son of God and today we can follow Him and speak with authority concerning the Word of God. He was the greatest Teacher of all times.

H. G. Wells said, in the *Readers Digest* a few years ago, "I have no theological advice, but no person can write a history of civilization or the progress of humanity without giving first and foremost place to a penniless Teacher of Nazareth." H. G. Wells was an atheist. He did not believe in God, but he said, "When I come to write history I must give first place to Jesus of Nazareth." Even the world recognizes and professes and admits that He was the greatest Personality ever to cross the stage of life. Even though they deny that He was God, refuse to believe that He was the Son of God, deny His deity, scoff at His resurrection and refuse to accept His virgin birth, they still recognize that He was the greatest Personage of all history and that He has had more effect on the world than any man that has ever lived.

I want you to see Jesus Christ at the end of His life. See Him as He is in the upper room and His followers are gathered around for the Last Supper. Suddenly a shadow passes across the face of the Lord Jesus. One of the disciples said, "Lord, what's wrong?" Then He looked up with sorrow in His eyes and said, "One of you is going to betray Me." They looked at each other horrified, hardly believing it. Who could it be? They started asking, "Lord, is it I?" "Lord is it I?" John, who had leaned upon His bosom said, "Lord is it I?" Peter, realizing the weakness of flesh said, "Lord, is it I?"

Then you remember that after this they went into the Garden of Gethsemane, and there the Lord Jesus began to pray. As He prayed, He said, "O Lord, if it be possible, let this cup pass from Me. O Father, if there is any other way to redeem the world, if there is any other way of salvation, if You can do it any other way, Lord do it." But in the providence of God and to fulfill the Word of God, the Lord Jesus was slain. He gave Himself because He loved you and me. There at Gethsemane the Lord Jesus said, "Nevertheless, not My will but Thine be done." The Lord Jesus was willing to endure suffering, was willing to have God turn His back, was willing to die because He loved us and did not want us to spend eternity in hell.

That night the soldiers came and Judas planted a little kiss on Christ's cheek and the soldiers seized Him and took Him off to the Sanhedrin. Later when Peter denied Him and the other disciples were fleeing, Jesus stood alone and was tried for His life and condemned. But the very confusion of the Sanhedrin shows me that Jesus Christ was innocent of every charge brought against Him by those false witnesses. The next day we find that He is taken to Herod and to Pilate. Pilate declares that He is innocent and takes a bowl of water and washes his hands in front of the whole multitude. Then Pilate said, "I am washing my hands of this just man." But, O Pilate, you will never wash the blood stain of Jesus Christ from your hands. You never will!

Tradition tells us that several years later Pilate was way up in the mountains of Switzerland by a little blue lake and those there with him saw him washing his hands. Somebody asked, "What are you doing, Pilate?" He said, "I am trying to wash the blood stain of Jesus Christ off my hands." Through all eternity Pilate will try to wash the blood stain off, but he can never do it.

Pilate's wife had said to him that day, "Have thou nothing to do with this just man." The court of man's conscience declared Him innocent. But in spite of Pilate's own feeling and his wife's warning, he stood before that multitude and asked "Which shall I release to you, Barabbas or Jesus which is called the Christ? The people yelled and clamored, saying, "Release Barabbas and crucify Jesus." They made their choice that day.

Tonight you will have to make your choice. Every man, every woman, every boy and every girl, whether you like it or not, you will have to make your choice between Barabbas and Christ,—between pleasure and Christ, between amusements and Christ, between popularity and Christ, between money and Christ. Whatever is keeping you from the kingdom of God, you will have to make a choice tonight and if you refuse to make the choice, the very act means that you will have already made it.

So they took Jesus away. They put a crown of thorns upon His brow; they put spikes in His hands and feet. Then they raised Him on a cross to crucify Him between heaven and earth.

One of the malefactors on the right hand turned to Him and said, "Lord, when thou comest to thy kingdom remember me."

Jesus replied, "Today shalt thou be with me in paradise." The people gathered about the cross, laughing and scoffing. "Today thou shalt be with me in paradise—what does He say?"

Finally He cried out, "It is finished." Then all of hell laughed, saying "Boy, we have got Him now. He claimed to be the Son of God, but now He is dead, He is finished, and He himself admits that He is finished."

A great artist painted a picture of the crucifixion of Jesus Christ. On the bottom of it he wrote, "Finished." Someone came along later and erased it and said, "Sir, we are going to put the word 'beginning' instead of 'finished' because redemption was finished, but life was begun in Jesus Christ."

When Jesus Christ died on the cross of Calvary, people were discouraged. The tragedy of His death rested heavily upon them. We see the silence of Saturday. That day the fearful disciples gathered together in an upper room. Thousands who had heard Him on Palm Sunday and welcomed Him to Jerusalem were now disappointed and disillusioned. We see two people walking along the road toward Emmaus, discouraged, disconsolate, disillusioned, fear grips their hearts. There had been no word from heaven, no miracles performed, nothing but death, and the awful, terrible silence. Jesus had said that He was going to rise from the dead, but they didn't really believe, and so now they were fearful and afraid. Silence and fear had gripped the people that once followed Him, the people that once believed in Him—His disciples, His apostles—they were all afraid and trembling. Saturday was an awful day. Those twenty-four hours must have seemed like an eternity as His friends waited, knowing not what might come.

Tonight, this old world is in fear. Tonight, this old city is in fear—the whole Nation is fearful. There are millions of little people in Europe who are afraid and filled with terror. They tremble because in Europe everyone knows that war is coming—war is inevitable. They know that they are not going to live a normal life. They know that the atomic bombs are going to start dropping and that Europe is going to be destroyed. Those people are living in daily fear, knowing that one of these days may bring the end—it may be any day. Our scientists said that Russia would not have the atomic bomb until 1953. They were three years off. They said, "We will not have war until 1955." If they were three years off in the atomic bomb, how much more off are they concerning war? I don't know. Nobody knows. That is all in the hands of a sovereign God. But there is one thing I know—people are afraid. People are afraid to die.

They are afraid of depression; afraid of old age; afraid of war—they are afraid of a thousand things.

This Nation is living by headlines—excitable, nervous, jumpy and afraid. You let a little earthquake come like it did a few months ago and people will get out on the streets and pray. Brother, I tell you, you want to start praying. One time I was on a plane six hundred miles over the Atlantic when the motor caught fire. Some of the passengers were playing cards, drinking cocktails, cursing and swearing and having a big time, but when that motor caught on fire, you couldn't find a card being played and you couldn't find anyone drinking whisky. Everybody on that plane was praying! Yes sir, one of these days we are going to start praying. We don't think about praying now, but we are going to think about it then. We don't think about dying now, but we are going to think about it then. We don't think about God now, but we are going to think about Him then, because one of these days God's judgment is going to come on this old wicked town. I don't believe there is a more wicked town in all the world than Los Angeles. One of these days the wrath of God is going to be poured out. Some of these people that laugh at prayer and revival meetings will change their minds. Brother, this old tent won't hold the people trying to get in. Those who now refuse Christ will come and the houses of God will be filled. You won't have to advertise in the newspapers; you won't have to spend money on the radio to get people in; you won't have to have spot announcements; you won't have to have big signs. Brother, they will be coming in swarms and droves and there will be overflow services in the biggest buildings in town. People will be trying to get to God, but I'm afraid their praying will be too late!

It was a fearful thing on Saturday as those disciples trembled and were afraid for they didn't know which way to turn. The world said, "Well, He's dead. He's out of the way. We won't be troubled with His preaching any more. This fellow that ate

with publicans and sinners, we won't be troubled with Him."
Old Caiaphas and Annas got together and they had a wonderful
time. They had a little cocktail party and celebrated. Christ is
dead; He's out of the way.

On Friday, Joseph of Arimathea had taken Christ's body,
lovingly and tenderly. Nicodemus had gone with him and together they put Christ's body in a tomb. The entrance to the
tomb was covered with a stone and sealed. Then Pilate sent
soldiers to stand guard, to be sure that nobody stole the body.

On Sunday morning, as the sun was rising on the eastern
horizon and the light was filling all the cracks and crevices
where the darkness had been a few moments ago, Mary and
Mary Magdalene came sorrowfully with tears streaming down
their cheeks. Their Lord and their Master was dead! They in-
tended to anoint His body with perfume and spices. When they
got to the tomb, they saw that something was wrong and then
they were more afraid than before. The stone had been rolled
away and they saw a man standing there. He was different
from any other man they had ever seen. Scripture says that his
clothes were like lighting. Did you ever see lighting flash? Just
hold the flash of lighting and you will see what the man looked
like that day. He was as brilliant as the noon-day sun, and the
women trembled and were afraid. This shining one said, "Be
not afraid," and then he gave the greatest message that has ever
been heard by any human ear. There has never been a message
comparable to the message that day, 2000 years ago, at the tomb
of Jesus Christ—"He is not here for he is risen, as he said."

If Christ had not risen, you and I would still be in our
sin and on the road to hell with never a chance of salvation.
The crux of Christianity is the resurrection of Jesus Christ. If
Jesus Christ be not risen from the dead, He's the biggest blas-
phemer that ever lived. If Jesus Christ did not rise from the
dead, He's a liar. He was not what He claimed to be. If Jesus
Christ is still in the grave, then there's no hope for any one of us.
When we die, everything is ended. We're through, if Jesus

Christ has not risen. This Bible is false and we might just as well throw it away. Jesus Christ is a liar. God has never spoken. We're just existing like so many puppets. We don't know why we're here, why we came, where we're going, if Jesus Christ is still in the tomb. But He has risen—the Bible says so and history declares it.

Do you remember when the war ended and the great slaughter was over? Remember that day when you heard that old Mussolini had given up the ship—a thrilling message that was flashed out across the air waves. Remember when Germany surrendered? Remember when Japan surrendered? What a thrilling day it was around the world when the news was flashed that Japan had surrendered and GI Joe started home! Brother, that's no news at all compared to the news proclaimed at the tomb of Jesus Christ when the angel said to Mary and Mary Magdalene, "He is not here; he is risen."

They looked in the tomb, but the body of Jesus was not there. They saw an empty tomb for Jesus Christ, the Son of God, lives! At the right hand of God the Father, the Lord Jesus Christ lives for ever more and He lives to make intercession for us. He's sitting there, not as God, but as the God-man, as much God as He was man, as much man as He was God. If you stood before Him tonight, you would see the nail prints in His hands. You'd see the scar in His side. You'd see the mark of the spike in His feet because the Lord Jesus has the same body. He rose bodily from the grave that day.

A lot of people would say, "I don't believe that." Do you believe George Washington lived? There's more proof that Jesus Christ rose from the dead than there is that George Washington ever lived. A couple of fellows got together some time ago. Both of them were skeptics. They said, "We're going to write on 'Why we believe Paul was never converted on the road to Damacus' and 'Why Jesus Christ never rose from the dead.'" So they spent a year in research and met again. Both had been converted! Littleton had written on the observations of Saul's conversion, proving that he was converted as the Scriptures said. West had written on the proof in history of the resurrection of Jesus Christ. Their research had convinced them that if you accept any other event in history, you must accept the bodily resurrection of the Lord Jesus Christ.

But we need no other proof than the Word of Almighty God. That's all the proof we need. I don't care what the scientist has to say. I'm not dependent on what the scientist tells me to believe about this Book. Every time some big shot scientist comes along and makes a statement complimentary to the Word of God we rush out and say, "Boy, look what so and so said—Look what Dr. so and so, a Ph.D. from Oxford, had to say." I don't care what any scientist says. The Word of God is enough. We don't need to depend on the world to tell us whether this is God's Word or not! God said so and we accept it by faith and believe it from cover to cover as God's inspired, holy Word and when God says that Jesus Christ, the Son of God, rose from the dead, bless the Lord, I believe it—every bit of it. But it can be proved from history.

One day a minister was talking to a brilliant lawyer. This lawyer said, "Sir, if you could prove to me that Jesus Christ rose from the dead, I would become a Christian. I cannot believe that Jesus Christ rose from the dead. I cannot believe that He came up out of that grave bodily and is living, but if you'll prove it to me, I'll become a Christian and live for Jesus Christ."

"All right," said this Presbyterian minister, "If I get you the proof that Jesus Christ rose from the dead you'll believe me?"

"Yes."

"All right, you come back one week from now and I'll have it."

He got all his figures and facts and statistics together and gave them to the lawyer. The young man studied the evidence for over six weeks. One day he came back and said, "Sir, here are all the things you gave me and thank you."

"What do you say? Did He rise from the dead?"

"Sir, I'm a lawyer and it has been proved to me beyond a shadow of a doubt that Jesus Christ rose from the dead."

"Then you'll become a Christian?"

"No sir, I don't think I can because I found out that my trouble was heart trouble instead of head trouble."

And that's the trouble today. The trouble is not with your head. I have fellows come up to me very often to say, "I have an intellectual doubt." Usually I tell them, "You come to Jesus Christ by faith and your intellectual doubt will flee."

But what does the resurrection of Jesus Christ mean to you and me? First of all, it means that Jesus Christ is what He claimed to be. That Jesus Christ was deity. That Jesus Christ was God incarnate. That Jesus Christ spoke the truth when He said, "I and my father are one" (John 10:30). And then the Lord Jesus Christ said He came to save us from sin. If we believe on Christ we shall be saved. He meant what He said and there is no other way of salvation except through Him.

Secondly, the resurrection means that God has accepted Christ's atoning work. Listen to this: "Who was delivered for our offences and raised again for our justification." God accepted Abel's sacrifice, but He rejected Cain's sacrifice. What would He do with the sacrifice of Jesus Christ upon the cross of Calvary? Would He accept it? Can we be saved through the sacrifice of Christ upon the cross of Calvary? How can we know? God said, "This is my Son in whom I am well pleased."

God turned His back and the Lord Jesus was separated from God for a space of time on the cross of Calvary, going to hell for our sins, suffering spiritually and physically, yet on the third day the Father loved the Son and because the Father also loved you and me, He accepted the finished work on the cross of Calvary. He raised up the Lord Jesus. When Jesus rose from the dead it was a living proof that anyone can be saved by the blood of Jesus Christ; by believing on the Lord Jesus Christ, accepting Him as your Lord and Saviour. Scripture says that you can be born again by accepting Christ as your Saviour. The Bible tells us that if we confess with our mouths the Lord Jesus and believe in our hearts that God has raised Him from the dead, we shall be saved. But you cannot be saved without believing in the resurrection of Jesus Christ! Unless He rose again, His death would mean no more than the death of any human martyr.

You know why the apostles and the early Christians were persecuted and beaten, stoned and thrown into the lion's den? Not for preaching the teaching of Jesus, nor the virgin birth. It was not for preaching His coming again, but for preaching the resurrection. Unbelievers couldn't stand the truth of the resurrection because if Satan can win the battle of the resurrection, he's won everything. Thanks be unto God, Satan never won the battle. It was won by the Lord Jesus when He died and was raised up by God from the grave. Now God says, "If you confess with your mouth the Lord Jesus and believe in your heart that God has raised Jesus, you're saved."

You say, "But what do you mean? I don't have to work for my salvation?" No.

"I don't have to pay for it?" No.

"You mean that I don't have to join anything?"

All you have to do is to believe in your heart that Jesus died for your sin and that God raised Him from the dead. Then confess with your mouth that Christ is Lord. The Bible says that you're saved and if you died, you would go straight to heaven.

You say, "But I'm not sure that I'm saved. I belong to the church. I live a pretty good life and all the rest of it but I'm not sure. I have a doubt." Your doubt can flee tonight by letting Jesus come into your heart and trusting Him as personal Saviour.

Next, His resurrection means that there is power for a victorious life. "That ye may know what is the exceeding greatness of his power to usward who believe, according to the working of his mighty power, which wrought in Christ, when he raised him from the dead." Scripture says that the same power, the same energy, the same atomic power of God that was used to raise Christ from the dead is the power that He gives me to live victoriously every day. Isn't that wonderful? We don't have to live lives of defeat. I don't have to go around with my head dragging the ground. I don't have to go around from defeat to defeat, wearing a black coat. I don't have to go around with a long face, but I can go around with a smile, with my shoulders back, realizing that I have been washed by the blood of Jesus Christ and adopted into the family of God and now am His son. I'm a member of the royal family of heaven by adoption into God's family. The same power that raised Christ from the dead gives me power to have daily victory over sin. Isn't that wonderful? The people who have peace in their lives are the people that know Jesus Christ. The only people that are truly happy in the world are the people that know Christ. The only people that have peace, joy and rest, and who are undisturbed by the events in the world are those that are in Jesus Christ!

The resurrection of Christ is a guarantee that our bodies, too, are going to be raised from the grave in that day that is yet to come. "But now is Christ risen from the dead and become the first fruits of them that sleep. For if we believe that Jesus died and rose again even so them also which sleep in Jesus will he bring with him."

One of these mornings we're going to have a great, glorious resurrection. You remember old Dad? Think of him when he went home to be with the Lord. See him, with tears coursing down his cheeks, as his trembling hand gripped yours and he said, "Good-by." Remember mother, dear sweet mother that used to sit in the rocking chair and rock you, the mother whom you loved, who prayed for a boy, a girl. Remember Mom; when you laid her away you thought your heart would break. Remember that loved one you laid away? Remember Jim, Bill,

Susie, Mary, whatever the name was. You laid them away in a grave. One of these days those old graves are going to pop open. The gravestone is going to be thrown out of the way and these loved ones will be raised to be with the Lord, and so shall they ever be with Him.

These who are raised will have new bodies—incorruptible and immortal. That is a wonderful thing to think about. I've had a lot of trouble with this old sack of bones I carry around. I don't think that I have very many days when I can say I feel good all the time. Some of us are limping around. I saw a dear brother on a crutch walking up here last night to sing his solo. I said to myself, "One of these days, that brother's old body is going to straighten out and he's going to rise from the grave, if the Lord should tarry, and he should die." Isn't that going to be a wonderful day? That resurrection morning our bodies are going to be raised and there will be no more tears, no more headaches, no more backaches, no more rheumatism, no more crippled bodies, no more sorrow, no more grief.

We're going to be raised to be with the Lord in the air. Scripture says that we're going to have a new body. I've never been able to sing down here, but I'm going to ask the Lord to let me sing up there. I have never been able to play the trombone or the violin. I have never been able to do some of the things that others do, but one day Scripture says I'll have a new body and I'll sing with the best of them and play with the best of them. I'll play as good football or baseball as all the rest of them because the Scripture says that I'm going to have a new body. Some of these dear gray-headed brethren that haven't been able to run in thirty years are going to start running and leaping and shouting and praising the Lord. Won't that be wonderful?

The Bible says that we are going to have a new body and we are going to be raised from the dead. And you know how I know it? Because God said that Jesus rose, and because Jesus rose, we're going to rise also.

What about you though—wait a minute. Don't say "Amen" too loud. You know what is going to happen? Some of you are not going to rise that day. You know why? Because the Scripture says only those that are asleep *in Christ* are going to rise at His coming and meet Him in the air. Unbelievers are going to be raised later—that is the resurrection of the damned. It will be a most awful resurrection. The damned are raised to face God in the great White Throne Judgment.

Scripture tells us about the land where we shall live forever. It tells us about the resurrection. Listen to this:

"And I saw a new heaven and a new earth: for the first heaven and the first earth were passed away; and there was no more sea. And I John saw the holy city, new Jerusalem, coming down from God out of heaven, prepared as a bride adorned for her husband. And I heard a great voice out of heaven saying, Behold, the tabernacle of God is with men, and he will dwell with them, and they shall be his people, and God himself shall be with them, and be their God. And God shall wipe away all tears from their eyes; and there shall be no more death, neither sorrow, nor crying, neither shall there be any more pain: for the former things are passed away. And he that sat upon the throne said, Behold, I make all things new" (Rev. 21:1-5).

Listen to this:

"And death and hell were cast into the lake of fire. This is the second death. And whosoever was not found written in the book of life was cast into the lake of fire" (Rev. 20:14, 15).

There are two resurrections—the resurrection of the Christians, the persons who accepted Christ, and the resurrection of the persons who rejected Christ. Those who rejected Christ will be raised to face the great White Throne Judgment and will be cast into the lake of fire and brimstone to spend eternity. Two places to spend eternity—one is the lake of fire and brimstone, spending eternity without God. Or one can have an eternal life of joy and happiness, streets of transparent gold, walls of jasper, palaces of ivory, gates of pearl, and, most important of all, the Lord Jesus will be there. There are two resurrections and two places to spend eternity.

Are you sure tonight that you're ready to meet God? Are you certain that you are saved? Listen, there is no second chance after death! There is no "if" in the Scriptures; no word that you can be saved one minute after death. God is now giving you a chance to trust in Jesus Christ as your Saviour and to know that you are saved, ready to meet Him, should he come tonight. Are you ready? Are you sure of it. Make sure. Make certain that you are ready to meet God and one day you will rise to be with Him in glory!

Judgment

"And the times of this ignorance God winked at; but now commandeth all men every where to repent: Because he hath appointed a day, in which he will judge the world in righteousness by that man whom he hath ordained; whereof he hath given assurance unto all men, in that he hath raised him from the dead" (Acts 17:30, 31).

ANOTHER passage of Scripture is found in Hebrews, "It is appointed unto men once to die, but after this the judgment" (Heb. 9:27). A young minister was sitting in his study. It was just after the evening service and he had preached on this passage of Scripture. There was a knock and a young man entered and said, "Sir, I should like to argue with you about a statement you made. First of all I do not believe that there is a God. Can you prove that there is a God? And, secondly, can you prove that the Bible is the Word of God?'

As the young fellow asked these questions, the minister gave only one answer—"It is appointed unto men to die, but after this the judgment."

"But sir, I came here to argue with you."

The minster replied, "It is appointed unto men once to die, but after this the judgment." The young man tried his best to argue with the minister, but the minister refused any dispute. Again and again he repeated this same verse and finally the young man went home. But all evening he thought of the minister's words. When he went to sleep that night he dreamed about them. During breakfast the verse was again in his thoughts. At his place of business he could almost hear the minister saying, "It is appointed unto men once to die, but after this the judgment." He went about the ordinary tasks of the day, but he thought continually of this verse, and he could see it, and even in his dreams he heard, "It is appointed unto men once to die, but after this the judgment." He came back to the minister and said, "Sir, I am convinced that the Bible is the Word of God, I am convinced that God exists and I am convinced that Christ is my Saviour and," he said, "I want to be saved right now and escape the judgment."

The Word of God is quick and powerful and sharper than any two-edged sword. The Word of God is more powerful than any illustration that I can use; it is more powerful than any story I could tell. The Word of God is a hammer; it is a sword and a mirror. And so tonight I want to turn to God's Word. There are many people who feel that there's a last, final, general judgment. You know, when I come to read and study the Bible I find that I must unlearn many things that I have learned. Some of the things I have been taught as a child or learned in school were not according to the Word of God. Tonight I want to describe the great White Throne Judgment the way I believe Scripture explains it. I believe that the Bible teaches of several and perhaps many judgments. I want to mention four of them.

The first is the judgment of sin that took place on the cross of Calvary more than 1900 years ago. Now when Christ died on the cross of Calvary, you as a Christian in God's reckoning, and in God's sight, died with Christ. Paul said, "I am crucified with Christ: nevertheless I live." And Paul also said to reckon ourselves dead indeed unto sin. On the cross of Calvary, the Lord Jesus Christ died in our stead as a substitute for our sins. Scripture says about the one who had his sins judged at Calvary, "hath everlasting life, and shall not come into condemnation; but is passed from death unto life" (John 5:24). I believe that Scripture teaches that Christians will not appear at the great White Throne Judgment. I shall never be there, thanks be unto God. There is therefore now no judgment to them that are in Christ Jesus, because the Lord Jesus Christ was judged, of His own will, sin in our stead. My sins were borne by Christ at Calvary and I'll never have to face them again. Satan may point his finger at me and say, "There's Billy Graham. Why, Billy Graham is a sinner! Look at the kind of life he leads. Look at all the lies he's told. Look at all the things he did when he was a boy."

But God says, "But the blood of Jesus Christ has cleansed Billy from every sin." You'll never be able to work your way into that position before God. You can't buy it. It's a free gift from God, the Father, through the Lord Jesus Christ.

When the Lord Jesus Christ said, "It is finished," that guaranteed to every believing child of God that the plan of salvation was completed. I can never work for it, I can never buy it, but I can receive it through belief in Christ.

The most awful, horrible, terrible judgment of all time took place at Calvary. The Lord Jesus suffered more when God turned away from Him than all the people in the world can ever suffer. When God judged the Lord Jesus Christ in your stead and in my stead, that judgment was so awful that Jesus said, "My God, my God, why has thou forsaken me?"

Then the second judgment is the judgment of self. I just want to mention it in passing. Unless we judge ourselves, God has to chasten us. Now notice in Scripture that God has two weapons, the first is the rod and the second is a sword. The Christian will never suffer the judgment of the sword. That is to be for the unrepentant sinner alone. God used the sword on Cain. That is the sword that He is going to use on the unbeliever. But God does use the rod on Christians. Do you know why God has to use the rod on us and spank us? Because we don't judge ourselves. We don't confess our sins; we go on backsliding and in grieving the Holy Spirit. Then God has to take the rod and paddle us and when God punishes us, it's not just a little light stroke, it hurts. Sometimes He leaves a bruise by His hand.

In the Corinthian church a man was living in a sinful relationship with his father's wife (I Cor. 5). That is to say his step-mother. He refused to judge himself and the church was directed by apostolic authority to hold a meeting in the name of our Lord Jesus Christ and with the power of our Lord Jesus Christ to deliver such a one unto Satan for the destruction of the flesh that the spirit might be saved in the day of the Lord Jesus. In other words, here was a man living in sin who refused to judge himself; refused to confess his sin and renounce it. Paul said, "All right deliver him over to the Devil and let the Devil strike him a few times." We find in II Corinthians 2:5-7 that this man was brought unto self-judgment and restored to perfect fellowship once again. Now God may find it necessary to let the Devil bring certain tribulation upon us. But there is a vast difference between tribulation and wrath. No believer need suffer the wrath of God because the Lord Jesus bore that for us at the cross.

We are told to judge ourselves. "For if we judge ourselves, we should not be judged" (I Cor. 11:31). Now what does that mean? You ought to confess your sin as soon as you realize you have done wrong. Don't wait for God to chasten you. The Lord has many ways of punishing His children. But God will mold you into the image of the Lord Jesus Christ. That is why it is so desperately important to have self-judgment. Judge yourself when you sin. Confess your sin. Renounce it or you are going to come under the chastening hand of the Lord. God has had to chasten me sometimes and He has had to chasten you. We don't like it for when we are chastened and disciplined of the Lord we are not walking with Him.

Perhaps you are saying, "Well I've been getting along pretty well. God hasn't bothered me yet." That doesn't mean that He's not going to bother you. That just means that He is long-suffering, not willing that you should be chastened. He is giving you a lot of room and He is giving you a chance to judge yourself. Don't think that because He hasn't chastened you yet, He never will. Brother, you don't know God. God chastens those whom He loves. He will punish if you as a

Christian keep on in your sins, your back-sliding and your wandering away from God. He'll chasten you just like He did Job. Job was a self-righteous man. He loved God, but failed to confess his sin. We have to read up to chapter 42 before we find Job realizing his own sin and saying, "I abhor myself."

Now the next judgment we come to is the judgment of works. Works can never be the grounds for our salvation, but once one becomes a Christian, work alone for Christ is part of our Christian growth and brings a reward.

> "For other foundation can no man lay than that is laid, which is Jesus Christ. Now if any man build upon this foundation gold, silver, precious stones, wood, hay, stubble; Every man's work shall be made manifest: for the day shall declare it, because it shall be revealed by fire; and the fire shall try every man's work of what sort it is. If any man's work abide which he hath built thereupon, he shall receive a reward. If any man's work shall be burned, he shall suffer loss: but he himself shall be saved; yet so as by fire" (I Cor. 3:11-15).

What does that mean? That passage of Scripture teaches us this: We cannot work for salvation—never. The Bible says, "For by grace are ye saved through faith; and that not of yourselves: it is the gift of God: Not of works, lest any man should boast." You can work in a woman's auxiliary all the rest of your life and die and go to hell. You can go to church every Sunday; read your Bible; pray three times a day; die and go to hell. You can live a good life and die and go to hell. The Bible says that you're not saved by works. The Bible says that you can't work your way to heaven, you can't buy your way to heaven. The Bible says that it's a free gift from God. But, after you're saved, after you believe and are born again by accepting Jesus Christ as your personal Saviour, you start working for the Lord Jesus Christ. What's the motive of your work? The motive is this, the love of Christ constraineth me.

The love of Christ constraineth me from the moment I accept Him as my Saviour. Fourteen years ago the love of Christ constrained me to work, to preach, and to go out and compel men to come to Jesus Christ. The Bible says we ought to be working and our main business on earth after we believe is to work for Jesus Christ.

If you are in the automobile business, the insurance business, whatever business you are in, that's secondary and should always have second place to your business of working for the Lord Jesus Christ.

The Scriptures describe the judgment seat of Christ, where Christians receive rewards for their works. One of these days the Christians, every person that has been bought with the precious blood of Jesus Christ and is living for Jesus Christ, is going to be caught up in the air and so shall we ever be with the Lord. But we who are Christians are then going to stand before the judgment seat of Christ. This has nothing to do with your salvation. This has nothing to do with your sin because your sin was judged at Calvary. You'll never be at the great White Throne Judgment. There is a distinction— at the judgment of Calvary Christ bore our sins; at the judgment seat of Christ believers receive rewards for the work that they've done for the Lord Jesus since the moment they believed.

Here is the way Paul describes the judgment seat of Christ:

"Wherefore we make it our aim, whether at home or absent, to be well pleasing unto him. For we must all appear before the judgment seat of Christ that everyone may receive the things done in his body, according to what he hath done, whether it be good or bad" (II Cor. 5:9, 10, R.V.).

"But why dost thou judge thy brother? or why dost thou set at nought thy brother? for we shall all stand before the judgment seat of Christ" (Rom. 14:10).

"Therefore judge nothing before the time, until the Lord come, who both will bring to light the hidden things of darkness, and will make manifest the counsels of the hearts:

and then shall every man have praise of God" (I Cor. 4:5).

"And, behold, I come quickly; and my reward is with me, to give every man according as his work shall be" (Rev. 22:12).

Now, at this judgment every believer will stand before Christ to receive his reward. Scripture says, "Every man shall have praise of God." I'm glad for that verse because it means that the humblest one of God's servants will be there. The dear woman who washed clothes to care for her family, and the child of God who has never done anything spectacular for the Lord.

Then we are to be given certain crowns. I am looking forward to wearing a crown in that day. There is the incorruptible crown, given to believers who separated themselves from the world and were separated unto God. There's a crown of rejoicing for the soul winner. That doesn't necessarily mean that it's the big evangelists who are going to get that crown. Sometimes people pat me on the back and say, "Boy, you're winning a lot of souls to Christ, you must be going to get a big crown." But listen, it's not how many souls you won; how big the meetings were that you had. It's whether you are faithful in the place where God puts you. If God puts you to selling automobile tires and you sell them faithfully as unto the Lord and witness for Christ at every opportunity; if He puts you to washing dishes and scrubbing floors, and you wash dishes and scrub floors faithfully as unto Him and witness, you'll get that crown. Or if God puts you to keeping house and raising children and you do it faithfully, you will have your reward.

Then there's the crown of righteousness which is given to those who are looking for His coming. The crown of glory goes to the faithful teachers and pastors. I'd like to say something. A lot of people say, "My, I wish we had a preacher like that evangelist. Wish we could get an evangelist to come into our church and stir the people and be our pastor." Listen to this: God through His Holy Spirit has given different gifts to believers—not only the gift of the evangelist, but there's the gift of a pastor, there's the gift of a teacher. There are various gifts which the Spirit of God has given to His Church and one gift is just as important as the other. Each one is to be done faithfully unto the Lord. I could never be a pastor because God didn't give me that gift. I have often prayed that God would give me that gift. God didn't give me the gift of a teacher. If God has given me any gift at all, I say it humbly and with glory to His name because He can take it away from me, He gave me the gift of an evangelist and wants me to be faithful in winning men to Jesus Christ and warning them to repent of their sin. That's my job. God has a crown and rewards for all those who are faithful.

Now listen to this:

> "The four and twenty elders shall fall down before him that sat on the throne, and worship him that liveth for ever and ever, and cast their crowns before the throne, saying, Thou art worthy, O Lord, and our God to receive glory and honour and the power for thou hast created all things, and for thy pleasure they are and were created" (Rev. 4:10, 11, R.V.).

In other words, when He hands me the crown, when He hands you the crown, and you put it on your head and it feels good and it sparkles and it looks good, you know what you're going to do? The Scriptures say that you're going to look at the Lord Jesus and you're going to realize that you didn't earn your crown. Then you're going to take it off and lay it at His feet and you're going to say, "Thou and thou alone art worthy to wear this crown." It was the Lord Jesus who bought us with His own blood on the cross of Calvary. I'm looking forward to that day. It is going to be a wonderful day. I can't wait!

Then we come last of all to the great White Throne Judgment. If you have ever listened to anything in your life, I want you to listen the next four or five minutes as I tell you what God says about this awful judgment. If you are outside of Christ, you're not a Christian, you never have accepted Christ as Saviour, you're not sure how you stand before God tonight, I want you to listen. No man or woman in this place tonight will ever be able to stand at that great White Throne and say I never knew—nobody warned me. You're going to be warned tonight and you're going to know tonight. I want you to see what God says. We read our passage of Scripture over again:

> "[God] now commandeth all men everywhere to repent: Because he hath appointed a day, in the which he will judge the world in righteousness by that man whom he hath ordained; whereof he hath given assurance unto all men, in that he hath raised him from the dead."

God says, "I have appointed a day." He announces it to the entire world. "Somewhere, sometime in eternity I am going to call everybody before Me and I'm going to judge them. Hear ye, hear ye, all the unbelieving peoples of the world are going to be judged in that day. Hear ye, movie stars of Hollywood, hear ye, presidents of the United States, hear ye, leaders and counselors of the world, hear ye peoples of the world, I have appointed a day in which I am going to judge the world by what you have done with Christ Jesus." Those are the words of the Lord God tonight.

In Noah's day, people laughed. They said, "Ha, judgment coming on the world? The old man's gone crazy! Why the old long-bearded fool, there's a screw loose somewhere. Talking about rain and a flood." They laughed at him, but the flood came. People laughed at Jeremiah. "Why the old crazy fellow. The old gloomy prophet just moaning all the time. Why the old fellow just sits around and moans and talks about a judgment coming and says that Jerusalem is going to be destroyed by Nebuchadnezzar. Ha, ha, ha, isn't that funny?" But Jerusalem was destroyed by Nebuchadnezzar.

They laughed at Lot. When Lot ran to the doors and

said, "Men of Sodom, men of Sodom, brimstone and fire are going to come down. Repent, repent. Get up and get ready."

"Ha, ha, leave us alone. Don't disturb us in our sleep. We're getting our good beauty rest. We don't want to be disturbed. Judgment coming!" They laughed and mocked and sneered, Scripture says, but Sodom was destroyed that night.

They laughed at Amos. The king sat on the throne and said, "Oh yea, you say prepare to meet God because judgment is coming and you say that the enemies of Israel are going to take Israel. Ha, why listen to me. We have our big battleships, we have big bombers and we have a B-36. We know we can defend our shores. We know that. And you old long-bearded country hick get back to the hills and start preaching, but don't come up here to scare us." Thirty years after this prediction was made, judgment came and the nation of Israel was scattered.

God Almighty, the same God that made predictions to those men—and every prediction came to fulfillment—says:

> "And I saw a great white throne, and him that sat on it, from whose face the earth and the heaven fled away; and there was found no place for them. And I saw the dead, small and great, stand before God; and the books were opened: and another book was opened, which is the book of life: and the dead were judged out of those things which were written in the books, according to their works. And the sea gave up the dead which were in it; and death and hell delivered up the dead which were in them: and they were judged every man according to their works. And death and hell were cast into the lake of fire. This is the second death. And whosoever was not found written in the book of life was cast into the lake of fire" (Rev. 20:11-15).

I want you to see that awful scene. The angels and archangels stand in attendance. At a place designated by Almighty God, Jesus Christ sits upon the throne. The angels are standing at attention. The heralds blow their horns and as the horns and the trumpets sound, the gates open and Hades releases all of the sinners who had been there. Here they come crying for the rocks to fall on them. Crying for the caves to open up and give them a place of hiding, for the mountains to shelter them, but there is no shelter, there is no hiding from Him that sits on the throne. From battlefields long since forgotten they come. Graveyards have given up the dead which lay there for hundreds of years. From the ocean depths where ships were sunken long ago they come. Millions and millions of them, the earth's great and little who played their parts upon the stage of life. They all come to stand before God at the great White Throne Judgment. If you are outside of Christ, if you've never taken Him as your Saviour, you'll be in that group. You'll be there and this is God's description and God's Word. Who's going to be the judge?

"The Father judgeth no man, [God is not going to judge] but hath committed all judgment unto the Son" (John 5:22).

Look at Him, as He sits on the throne. That can't be Jesus. Look at the fire coming from His eyes. Look at the sword coming from His mouth. That can't be my Lord Jesus, but I look closer and I see the scars in His hands and I see the place where they put the spear in His side and I see the scars in His feet, and I say, "That's Jesus! I knew Him as Saviour down yonder, but now He is judge and He sits on the judicial throne of the universe—not in mercy nor love, but in judgment. His holiness is flaming against the sins of the world."

You say, "Can that be?" It's God's Word. I'm just giving you God's Word tonight.

I look into that crowd and I see Caiaphas, the High Priest. I see Pilate, the Roman governor, I see the soldiers that put him to death. There is Judas Iscariot who sold Christ for thirty pieces of silver. I see Joe Stalin and Adolph Hitler; kings, presidents, princes, movie stars and actors who are known from coast to coast, but who refuse to accept Jesus Christ as Saviour. I see all the peoples of the earth and they stand before God

Almighty in that awful day and they cry for mercy, but there is no mercy! These all had their chances on earth, now it's too late! I think the saints of God are going to be there. Not in front of Christ, but standing behind Him because Scripture says, "Do ye not know that the saints shall judge the world?" (I Cor. 6:2). I think we are going to sit with Christ in that day—all those who accepted Him. Those who were despised on earth and scoffed at during their lifetime. Can't you see those old Roman emperors who caused Christians to be burned to death, standing there trembling and calling out for mercy? The Christians whom they burned to death are sitting on the throne with Christ and judging them. Can't you see those scores of Christians who have been put to death in Russia in the last 25 years standing there in judgment with Christ. Stalin will be there and all of the other international tyrants will be brought before Christ. They may bow the knee and their tongues may confess, but it will be too late! The time for mercy has passed—there is only judgment now. Who's going to be judged? Those outside of Christ. You know what happens when a Christian dies? That Christian goes immediately into the presence of the Lord. "To be absent from the body is to be present with the Lord."

Now listen, if you read in the paper tomorrow morning that Billy Graham was killed in an automobile accident because of someone's wild driving, you can just put it down that he's with the Lord. But this was not always so. Before Christ died, a Christian who died went to Paradise. Paradise was a compartment of Hades and that's the story that Jesus told about the rich man and Lazarus. Lazarus was in paradise; the rich man was in the part called Hades and they could see each other, but the gulf was too wide to reach one another. But listen, when the Lord Jesus Christ died on the cross of Calvary, He went to paradise. He said to the thief on the cross, "Today thou shalt be with me in Paradise." Jesus went to Paradise and led captivity captive. He opened the gates of the grave and opened the gates of Hades and let out of Paradise all the saints of all the ages. Today Paradise is with the Lord. Any Christian who dies now goes to be with Christ. But the unconverted, un-regenerated, hell-bound sinner is still in Hades—he's not in hell yet. The moment that a sinner dies, he goes to Hades. The final place of the sinner will be the lake of fire and brimstone. In that day of judgment, the spirit of the sinner is going to be brought out of Hades, reunited with the body from the grave. There will be the resurrection of the dead. All the dead will be brought to the great White Throne Judgment. Then each sinner who rejected Christ will be given his assigned place in the lake of fire and brimstone which the Scripture says burns forever. You say, "I don't like that." I'm telling you what God says; if you don't like it, you don't like what He says, not what I say. I'm giving it to you straight from God's Word.

Now, what kind of judgment is it going to be? It's not going to be any class judgment—not just the rich people or just the poor people. It's not going to be just the black people or just the red people. It's going to be the whole world. You know, you may make and break appointments here on earth, but that's one appointment you're going to keep. You won't be late to that meeting. You might be late to this meeting and you might get fidgety when the preacher goes over nine o'clock, but you're going to stay there at that judgment until you hear your sentence. Everything else will be forgotten. The places of amusement will be empty; the wheels of industry will have ceased turning. In that day the only thing that matters is what did you do with Jesus.

You may escape the officers of the law down here. You may go ahead and speed down the street or you may go commit a crime and get away with it and nobody ever catch you, but remember in that day your works will be known. God's officers never lost a man. The infidel will be there, some church members, drunkards, the idolaters, the one who has committed adultery, every sinner who has never confessed Christ will be there, the Scriptures say. They will all be judged and not a one of them will be able to object.

Then the books of God are opened and the dead are judged out of those things which were written in the book. God has a set of books and the Bible says, that you are going to be judged out of those things that God is writing in those books. God has your history from the cradle to the grave in that book, your every thought, every deed. God says He's going to open that book. What an awful thing when He opens that book. That book will prove that there's none righteous, no not one. The book is going to prove that all have sinned and come short of the glory of God. "The wages of sin is death . . . and the soul that sinneth, it shall die." Some people will say, "But oh Lord, I'm a church member."

"Here's the book," God will reply.

"But, oh Lord, I was a deacon."

"Here's the book."

"I was a Sunday school teacher."

"Here's the book."

"I was a good moral person."

"Here's the book."

And God is going to have proof of everything you ever did. He will know about that night years ago which you've forgotten. Every idle word that we have said—every curse word, every swear word, every lie, will all be recorded in His book. All those things that you covered up and hid as secret, God says, are going to be brought to life and the whole world will know and you'll stand there with perspiration dripping down your cheeks and with your eyes rolling in fear. Every one of us has done wrong, Scripture says, except the Lord Jesus Christ.

Next the roll will be called. The Lamb's Book of Life will be opened. I've been standing there listening as one after another was condemned because of sin. I know that I'm a sinner, and that I deserve the lake of fire and brimstone, but because

Christ was judged in my stead, He took my sin, I know that my name is in His Book of Life.

They start calling the roll of the saints and the saints start marching in. They read off the G's and then they come to Billy Graham. He deserves hell, he was a sinner, he was lost, he ought to spend eternity in the lake of fire and brimstone, but back yonder in 1935 he said "Yes" to Jesus Christ, the Son of God, and on the strength of the shed blood of Christ can spend eternity with God. His name was written in the Lamb's Book of Life 14 years ago.

You know, they can call me a fool if they want to; they can laugh, sneer and mock all they want to, but I'm glad I'm on the road to heaven. I'm glad that when the Lamb's Book of Life is opened, I'll be in that list.

What about you? What does a man go to hell for? Not for getting drunk, cursing, committing adultery, or lying. The only thing that will send a man to hell is rejecting Jesus Christ. The question on the judgment day will be "What did you do with Jesus." God knows that you have a chance right now to accept His Son as Saviour. What are you going to do with it?

> "When the great business plants of our city
>   Shall have turned out their last finished work,
>   And when the merchants have sold their last order
>   And dismissed every last tired clerk,
>   When our banks have raked in their last dollar
>   And have paid out their last dividend,
>   When the Judge of the earth wants a hearing
>   And asks for a balance—What then?
>
> "When the choir has sung its last anthem
>   And the preacher has voiced his last prayer,
>   When the people have heard their last sermon
>   And the sound has died out in the air,
>   When the Bible lies closed on the altar
>   And the pews are all empty of men,

When each one stands facing his record
And the great book is opened—What then?
"When the actors have played their last drama
And the minute has made its last span,
When the movie has flashed its last picture
And the billboard displayed its last ad,
And gone out in the darkness again,
When the trumpet of ages has sounded
And we stand before Him—What then?"

THE END

PACIFIC GRACE MISSION
CHAPEL
FRANCES ST. & WOODLAND DR.